PRAISE FOR *BETTER PARENTING*

"*Better Parenting* is an inside look at the critical issues that Somali parents in the diaspora are facing daily, and at the same time provides practical solutions to them specifically and the community in general."

—*Mustafa Ibrahim, PhD, executive director of STEP Academy Charter School*

"Having served on the elected Board of Directors of the Cedar Riverside Community School with Ruqia, I know she has valuable insight from all her years working with parents and children, helping them navigate US culture while parenting, that has led to her desire to raise awareness of current parenting issues and provide a parenting concept in the Islamic tradition. Ruqia is uniquely experienced to offer this guidance as a result of her education (both Islamic training and a Child Development degree) combined with her firsthand experience as a mother, navigator, and advocate working with parents and families. *Better Parenting* is a needed resource that will inform and support Somali parents."

—*Merrie Benasutti, Coordinator for Community Partnerships, Office for Public Engagement, University of Minnesota*

"I am pleased to see this thoughtful and scholarly work from Ms. Ruqia Abdi. There is a clear need in our community to bring well-researched insight about our community, from our community. Ruqia is well known and well respected as a thought leader regarding East African–Minnesotan youth. The success of our community will be dependent upon our ability to organize systems that build the capacity of families to guide our next generation toward our faith and civic ideals. Ms. Abdi, in her work, demonstrates that this effort cannot be done in isolation and cannot be done effectively without building right relationships with mainstream institutions such as healthcare, education, and government. Ms. Abdi should be seen as a trusted resource for both our families and systems that look to support those families."

—Sharif Mohamed, Imam of Islamic Civic Society of America and Open Path Resources

Better Parenting

A Guide for Somali Parents in the Diaspora

RUQIA ABDI

ISBN 13: 978-1-63489-191-2
Library of Congress Catalog Number: 2018967085
Printed in the United States of America
First Printing: 2018

22 21 20 19 18   5 4 3 2 1

Wise Ink Creative Publishing replaces every tree used in printing their books by planting thousands of trees every year in reforestation programs. Learn more at wiseink.com.

This book is dedicated to my children,
who are the vehicles of all my creative and
community-caring efforts. My compassionate
and caring daughter Sumaya, my service-minded
and easygoing son Khalid, and my lovely and
smart daughter Amina—I love you all! I will
continue to create an environment where you all
can have fun while being loved and nurtured!

This book is both cultural education and an
appreciation of the environment and knowledge
you will gain. You are all talented and fortunate
to have so many opportunities, and I hope you
will appreciate what you have and pay it forward
by helping others who are in need of help!

Contents

Introduction

Given my knowledge of child development, I have read and seen many recent parenting books on the market. However, I have not seen a book that rings true with my East African community or the parenting needs of the current Somali community. This book will shed light on the existing parenting challenges that East African, especially Somali, parents face in the diaspora, while pointing out some basic facts about Islam and our children's needs in the diaspora.

Whether you are a parent/caregiver, schoolteacher, dugsi Qur'an teacher, Maclin after-school teacher, or coach, you will find this book useful.

During my long years of working with parents and their children, I gained valuable insights into the needs of my community and how Somali parents struggle to raise their children in this new environment. The education that these parents need is called *parenting*, and I know many of my Somali friends will question this because the term gives them nightmares. The only time they hear this is when a child protection agency knocks on their door.

I used to get angry whenever I heard that all of a sudden the child protection agency wanted to take away the children of parents I knew to be excellent.

While I was working on my child development degree, I learned that there is a whole process that should take place before a child protection agent steps into somebody's home. I decided I would facilitate and present this parenting topic for Somali parents in an easy and relevant way, and in their language.

This book is not a solution to the problems facing the Somali parents and their children living in the United States or any other country in the world. Instead, it will raise awareness of current parenting issues and provide a basic concept of parenting in the Islamic tradition, as well as an overview of some child development theories. Raising children is a shared responsibility; as it is said, "It takes a village to raise a child."

This book will be like a toolbox, and you will use only the topics you need when you need them. I intend to make parenting as enjoyable and as rewarding as possible. The topics in this book are intentionally chosen, as they are being discussed among Somalis a lot!

CHAPTER ONE

Begin the Journey

To begin or not to begin, that is the big question! Parenting is a process, and if we do not start the process, we will not understand the concept of parenting at all.

In this chapter, we will explore the process of parenting in general, and then focus mainly on parenting in the Somali and Islamic culture. We will talk about how Somali parents of the diaspora have approached parenting and the challenges they have faced. The chapter will conclude with a discussion about the wave of change that shook the parenting habits and traditions of Somali parents.

What Is Parenting?

Every society has specific ways of raising children. These techniques may be rooted in customs, tradition, and religion. However, when we define parenting, there is no doubt that the way we approach it has a substantial effect on how children behave and learn.

First, let us see some definitions of parenting. Parenting is the process of upbringing a child according to one's culture and experience.

"Parenting style is considered a characteristic of the parent that is stable over time and constitutes the environmental and emotional context for child-rearing and socialization" (*Parenting Characteristics*).

When we hear the word *parenting*, especially among the Somali community, it describes what happens when the child protection agency gets involved and parents are asked to attend classes about parenting. In fact, parenting is something that is also familiar to students in higher education as well. We learn about different parenting styles in child development and education courses.

In the 1960s, Diana Baumrind researched how some parents interacted with their preschool children. After finishing her observation, she documented that there were three parenting styles that the parents used. These styles were authoritarian, authoritative, and permissive. Authoritarian means demanding complete submission; in other words, an authoritarian is like a dictator in a country where people do not have a say in anything. Authoritative parents are demanding, engaging, and accepting. They are also flexible and behave in a democratic way. Permissive parents give permission and are more concerned with friendship than following standards. The techniques involved with each parenting style give us a view of how each style impacts the behavioral and academic outcomes of children.

Authoritarian and authoritative parents are both strict and give children rules. The difference is that authoritarian parents are not responsive or sensitive, while authoritative parents are responsive. For example, authoritarian parents order the child to do something without explanation and expect complete obedience, while the authoritative parents order the child to do what they want but explain the reason behind the request. Permissive parents demand less and respond highly to the needs of children. A parent who practices this style sets out rules but does not use their parental authority to enforce those rules. They ask children if they can follow the rules, and if they do not, there is no consequence. Parents allow children what they ask for, when they ask for it, focusing more on pleasing children than on guiding them.

Children who are raised with a permissive parenting style perform well in school at times but not as well as others. They develop confusion on the limits of what they can do due to the inconsistency of rules they learned from their parents. They are also prone to drug use and delinquent behavior.

In the 1980s, two other psychologists, Eleanor Maccoby and John Martin, added a fourth parenting style called neglectful or uninvolved.

You will recognize neglectful parents from their behavior towards their children. They fail to provide a child's basic needs. These needs include food, clothing, safe shelter, and so on.

"Neglectful parents are neither demanding nor responsive" (Klein and Ballantine 2001, 46). Neglectful parenting might result from mental illness or other situations happening in the home like domestic abuse or financial problems.

We've seen the different parenting styles, and hopefully we can recognize our style and enhance or adopt a new one. We must also become conscious about our behavior toward our children because that determines how they will behave and approach the world around them.

Culture Shock Caused the Parenting Crisis

The majority of Somali immigrants came to the United States around 1993 from refugee camps. This was the result of the civil war that happened in 1991 after the Siad Barre regime was overthrown. According to Pew Research, the "U.S. is home to about 7% of the world's Somali migrant population" (Connor and Krogstad 2016). Minnesota is home to many of them, but others live in Columbus, Ohio; Seattle, Washington; and Virginia, or are scattered throughout other states in smaller numbers. In Minnesota, Somalis are thriving in terms of political participation and business, but there are some parenting issues that have resulted from the education system and are ruining the lives of the younger generation who either were born here or are growing up here!

The parenting crisis that exists among the Somali community is divided into two parts: one part resulted from the mistrust of Social Services, and the other from a lack of understanding of the education system, including parenting education. Lack of parenting education becomes apparent when a child reaches their teen years. Most Somali parents make strong connections between the new host country's culture and their teen's behavior.

Yes, there is cultural difference, but that has nothing to do with how the teen is behaving.

Apart from the social service that families receive, like health-care, housing, and food stamps, the first place that families interact when they come to the United States is the school. The reason is that education is compulsory; you do not have the choice to wait until you settle down and learn the culture of the host country.

When children start attending school but haven't adjusted, they might exhibit signs of neglect or abuse, even if that's not what's happening. Now the nightmare begins for parents. They receive a phone call from the school, and the interpreter tells them that they need to attend a meeting with the child's teacher and a social worker. As part of this process, the social worker contacts the child protection agency, and the parents start panicking, thinking that their child is going to be taken away from them.

One may argue that there is an interpreter or liaison to let parents know what the issue is, or is going to be, before the situation escalates to the child protection agency. However, the reality is that there is a gap in the information that reaches the parents.

Parents need education about the system and an interpreter or liaison who is bilingual and bicultural. The social worker also needs to be bilingual and knowledgeable of both cultures before jumping to conclusions.

Parents do not like or appreciate social workers due to negative communications they have had with them. Social workers mostly request a meeting with parents when the child reaches three or has unexcused absences, or when there is suspected child abuse.

Overview of How Somalis Raised Children Back Home

To understand any current condition of an issue, we must first examine how the problem evolved. As we pointed out, societies have their own child-rearing practices and ways of life. The method of living for Somali people was different back home. Raising children was a shared responsibility. Since Islam is the practiced religion in Somalia, parenting was considered to be upbringing and education, also known as Tarbiyah. Some of the parenting issues that confuse people, including the new Somali generation, stem from customs in Somali culture that have no basis in Islam. These issues include beating children, practicing female genital circumcision, and treating boys and girls differently.

In Somalia, mothers and fathers had different roles, and the extended family members were the support system. Extended family members include aunts, uncles, grandmothers, and grandfathers from the side of the mother and the father. If, for example, the mother wanted to go to a wedding, visit a friend who just gave birth, etc., an extended family member would come home to take care of the young ones. This family member could be an aunt, a niece, or grandmother. Sometimes neighbors would fulfill this role when a family member was not available.

Somali fathers were mostly the breadwinners for the family, and the mother stayed at home and cared for the children. There were some cases where the mother became the breadwinner. If the mother was divorced or the father passed away, mothers had to go to work. There were also some families where both parents worked while an extended family member or a paid nanny took care of the children. Older children used to go to schools or private tutors to receive a cultural education.

In schools, or dugsi, teachers were regarded as second parents. Children respected the teachers, and if problems happened, parents and teachers resolved it according to the situation. Education is a priority for Somali people, and they do whatever they can to make sure their children receive a high-quality education. There were also some rules and regulations that governed how children should be treated and protect their rights. These rules came in handy when child abuse happened, and they applied to anyone who cared for children, including extended family members.

So, it does "take a village" when we take a glance at the story of the old ways of Somali parenting. Social workers, counselors, and daycares were not necessary in most cases. Neighbors, extended family members, parents, and teachers acted as a support system for the family, and parenting felt so smooth and enjoyable! In the diaspora, by contrast, extended family members have to go to work or school, the neighbor might be totally unfamiliar to you in terms of culture or ethnicity, and the teacher is from a different culture and does not necessarily agree with you or the famous saying you hold dear: "It takes a village to raise a child."

So, for Somali people, there is a change that occurred on both the cultural side and the context side. People had to go through circumstances such as the civil war, and those experiences left some scars or trauma. In the diaspora, family members may not be the same as they used to be, and there are several cases of child abuse committed by close family members. Parents then feel ashamed to share the abuse with authorities due to stigma.

Emerged Parenting Challenges in the Diaspora

"Raising children is challenging. Our mothers did not playfully raise us." This statement is what I hear from Somali mothers whenever we discuss the parenting crisis that Somali parents are facing in the diaspora, especially in the United States.

It is essential to understand that the challenges these parents are referring to are different than the problems that emerged in the diaspora. In Somalia, parents faced two challenges: lack of educational opportunity and the means to feed their children. Mothers had to be the breadwinners for their children once a divorce happened because the majority of Somali husbands neglect the first wife. However, my aim is not to discuss whether that is due to Islamic or Somali social customs.

But in the diaspora, when we hear about parenting challenges in the Somali community, we are talking about three issues: lack of understanding of the education system, lack of trust in Social Services, and lack of a support system.

The Education System

The education system is the first thing parents get confused about, and it creates a long-lasting mistrust toward the rest of the services they receive from their host country!

After arriving in the United States, parents are supposed to enroll their children in schools. In school, the culture shock begins! Somali people have an oral tradition, and they communicate effectively face-to-face. When new parents enroll their children at a new school, the other parents give them a pep-talk about their experience in the education system.

Of course, there are interpreters and liaisons at the school, but the reality is, there is not a good relationship between parents and teachers. Parents start developing fear of the teachers' and social workers' questions because they are afraid their children will be taken away from them if the answer does not line up with American norms.

There is a missing link here. The bilingual liaisons that work at the schools the majority of Somali students attend are good at interpreting from English to Somali and vice versa during parent/teacher conferences and when conflicts occur. Parents, however, are only receiving directions and listening to what is happening while remaining unaware of their rights as parents and what they can contribute to this institution where their children spend at least seven hours a day. Yes, parents need help and need parenting classes, but teachers are also contributing to the communication gap that exists.

We have a very large number of Somali students in the Minneapolis and St. Paul area school districts, and we also have a growing number of Somali professionals and paraprofessionals joining the field in addition to interpreters and liaisons who work for the districts. The St. Cloud district seems to be showing the presence of Somali students more than Minneapolis and St. Paul due to race and discrimination issues (Mitchell 2016). The latter districts had discrimination issues against Somali students. So, parents are in a dilemma and are trying to go from school to school to seek quality education for their children. Some folks interpret the frequent moving and changing of schools as either proof of parents' lack of adjustment to the culture or the nature of Somalis' nomadic culture. The reality is that parents are looking for a good environment and quality education.

In education, if we want students to be successful, there should be open communication between parents and teachers as well as an understanding of the education system.

Teachers, on the other hand, cannot be successful in teaching these students without cultural competency training. This cultural knowledge is extremely important to start in early childhood settings to create a fresh and welcoming environment for all family members.

Teachers should know "about the social and cultural contexts in which children live—referring to the values, expectations, and behavioral and linguistic conventions that shape children's lives at home and in their communities that practitioners must strive to understand in order to ensure that learning experiences in the program or school are meaningful, relevant, and respectful for each child and family" (National Association for the Education of Young Children 2009).

One of the significant results of a lack of understanding of the education system is the efforts of some parents to send their children back home to learn the culture, a practice known as Dhaqan-Celis. This is the experience many parents want for their children, but some parents have nightmares because their children did not make it back home to Minnesota alive. Others are going back and forth, reconsidering their entire way of raising children. What is the solution, and what caused this massive issue of defining a successful education based on location and context? There is undoubtedly a wave of change that parents need to carefully learn from to accept that the world has changed!

Early childhood education is another issue in which parents need support and understanding. Young children need a holistic approach from the whole community while the parents are the primary teachers and decision makers for their children.

Trusting Social Services is an issue that stems from the school experiences of parents. It is also a barrier that Somali families encountered in the diaspora. Somali people go through lots of challenges as immigrants and refugees, most of them resulting in a dysfunctional family life. Most Somali parents do not seek family support and counseling services that are available for them. Parents are scared of what will happen if authorities find out about some of the behavioral problems that are happening at home.

This feeling—combined with language barriers—shuts parents out from communication with authorities. You may think that there are translators available to help them communicate. Firstly, the Somali community functions in the tribal system, so when a member of your tribe is the translator, to express everything is not welcomed! Also, if the parents are about to report sexual abuse, for example, it is taboo in the community, so they will swallow back their feelings.

Somali parents lack culturally sensitive services that will serve, educate, and help them, without judging them about their states caused by trauma, mental illness, a lack of education, and culture shock! I have heard many horror stories from Somali parents panicking because their children are going to be in the hands of a child protection agency! I worked in a school for several years and developed a mistrust toward the child support system and social workers because they made my neighbors and friends cry!

During my study of child development, I learned that there are processes that parents go through before their children are taken away due to abuse and neglect. One of these is education and information for the parents. I thought to myself, *This is cool, but why did I not see this process or hear about it from my friends?* So, understanding the education system is imperative for Somali parents.

Support Systems

A lack of a support system is one of the issues faced by Somali parents in the diaspora. I spoke with several Somali parents about the particular challenges they are facing in raising children and the difference between now and then. The answers I received revolved around the lack of a support system and a lack of understanding of the educational system due to a language barrier and trust issues. One of the parents, Nasro Noor, who has lived here for about 15 years, shared with me that life is hard when you are raising a child here. "I had to leave my baby with a babysitter, go to school, and go to work. It goes on and on, especially when you think about families back home; you sacrifice the time you should spend with your children."

As we pointed out, in Somalia, raising children was almost everyone's business. The extended family members notably acted as a social support system that glued the family together. Here, we see single mothers who never really handled school, a house, and health issues alone. Language is another considerable barrier that these mothers face within the diaspora. When mothers want to go to the hospital, for example, they need someone to help them care for their children. When they go to the hospital, they cannot say everything they feel, maybe because the interpreter is a male, so they leave the hospital without conveying what they wanted to.

A lack of support from the community and the society is evident from the lives of Somali parents.

Understanding the Wave of Change

You may say, why do we even need to learn to parent when we ARE already doing the job of parenting? You may be doing it exactly how your mother raised you because you watched her and want to repeat how she did things.

But we are now living in different times. Even in college, if you are taking the same sociology course that your mother took ten years ago, chances are the school is using different textbooks because the knowledge is getting updated every year. Some of the basic principles may stay the same, but many types of research might be outdated, with new ideas and cultural competencies out there. So, if you want to pass that sociology class, you will need a different textbook.

Now, let us say we are working for a particular organization that does not want to keep up with the needs of the society. The agency may stay with its old ideas, and the employees who agree with those early thoughts will remain with the company. However, organizations that want to survive and thrive will come up with ways to sync with their employees' byways of high-quality professional development and training, as well as activities that help them transform into productive and healthy individuals. We must do the same as parents.

Somalia had a civil war in 1991, and the internet was not on our radar, let alone the social media that we are using today. Our children are now growing up in a society that is changing quickly regarding technology, so school and work environments are not the same as they used to be.

We tend to believe that social media is what causes problems today. Before we talk more about the techno-logical advances that are happening at a faster rate, let us first see when some of the famous social media started (Shah 2016):

- Facebook launched in 2004.
- YouTube began in 2005.
- Twitter launched in 2006.
- Instagram launched in 2010.
- Snapchat launched in 2011.

So, technological change is real, and Snapchat is ev-erywhere, with children all over the world using it.

Now, before we say children in the United States are always on Snapchat and Facebook, thinking when they go back home to Somalia they will not use it, consider how integrated social media is in their lives.

Everything has bad and good sides; focusing on pos-itive aspects of using social media can alleviate some of our worries. Connecting online can benefit our children in many ways. They can do their homework and get help when they need it. You, as a parent, can help your chil-dren organize study groups where they can connect with each other at certain times and do homework, and if they are stuck on some topics you can direct them to YouTube video clips or an app if you do not know the answers yourself.

"Connectivity can also benefit family life. For in-stance, it's easy to stay connected with extended family" (Heitner, p.9). Let your children connect and chat with extended family members. What is better than getting sheeko xariir (stories) from a grandmother who lives in a faraway land, or learning a cultural class from a teacher that lives in another area!

Let us look at two of the mentioned social media sites and how people use them. Snapchat is very popular among middle and high schoolers. It is a social media app that allows you to chat, text, and send snaps, pictures, and videos. Each time friends exchange snaps, their streak gets higher. You may hear a teenager saying to their mother, "I want to do my streak when it is time to turn in the phone." You may see a fire emoji and number next to their friends; the numbers indicate how many days they've had contact, and the emoji means that the friends sent snaps twice in a 24 hour period. So streaks are so important. Finally, you can share stories in Snapchat, and they disappear after 24 hours.

Facebook, on the other hand, is an app that is popular among adults and some teens. It is an app that allows you to link videos, create pages, and share what you want with the world. Facebook uses the Messenger app for texting with friends privately. People in organizations or institutions use Facebook to create events and invite people to attend.

The possibilities of social media are endless. As a parent, you can learn the risks and benefits so you know what is going on and can step in when things go wrong. You can always get small video clips from YouTube on topics that you need to understand quickly. If you want to learn a little deeper, get a few other parents and request a workshop in your own language from your local library or education or community center.

Something else that I would like to recommend to parents is learning the legal aspects of using social media. Talking to your child about the risks of being online is also very important and establishes a trust between the two of you. You can start by telling them about how digital tracking can impact their future career if they are engaged in posting inappropriate things. Their own friends can sometimes post something about them or manipulate their picture just to ruin their dignity. Some children commit suicide because of harassment they encountered online.

For example, in Minnesota, it is a crime to share someone else's inappropriate pictures without their permission. You can also contact your local police and ask them what to do if you have a sensitive issue regarding social media that is impacting your child's life. Remember, just because we do not see people on the other side of the screen does not mean they cannot hurt the feelings of our children. There is bullying and harassment that happen online as well as offline.

There are many things our children do on social media, and it's our duty as parents to learn and help them be safe. There are some necessary aspects of social media that we have to master like what apps are safe, what apps are good for learning, and what apps pose a risk for cyberbullying. Yes, similarly to the real world, children are prone to fall for bullying behavior and predators when they are online and need our help to both save them and help them report any suspicious activity that makes them uncomfortable!

Ask your school teacher or a librarian to be a guide and help protect you and your children's privacy online.

We as parents are responsible for the well-being of our children. We are advocates, educators, and mentors. Yes, we need help to accomplish the goal of raising a responsible and productive individual. However, when something happens to that child tomorrow, and the child protection agency interferes, we, parents, are the ones crying. In Islam, we are held accountable if we fail to raise our children well.

We've learned that parenting is a process and that there are certain challenges that exist. We have also learned that parenting is a responsibility, and as parents we are held accountable if we fail the task of parenting. Next, we will explore the process of being effective parents as children move through different ages and stages of learning!

Understanding Types of Parents

Somali parents are in need of support and services including education, but unlike other parents, their need is slightly different depending on their arrival and generation type. I identified three types of parents after spending time around, observing, and interacting with them. The groups are: the catch-up, the cool, and the confused. In other words, some families are kind of confused, some are cool, and some are catching up!

The confused parents are those that came earlier and had children here. These parents are caught in between old cultural traditions and the new host country's culture. They try to educate their children the same way their parents raised them. Children of these parents need extra help and motivation when it comes to schooling. Parents have to remind them about their homework, especially in the teen years. The confused parents in the diaspora are in need of many services that help them understand the new system, learn the shortcomings of their perceptions, and survive with the trauma from the war-torn country they left.

The cool parents are those in the second generation. These young parents are the children of the confused parents and learned the hard way how life in their new country is different from their parents' culture. These parents are cool and try to get the highest quality education they can for their young ones. They learned the value of education and attended college. New parents in the cool generation usually accept parenting classes more than the confused and the catch-up!

The catch-up parents are the recent arrivals who probably arrived in the country during the last one to three years. Some of them have teens who are too old to be in regular high school or start high school, and graduation seems impossible due to the language barrier. They usually go to the credit recovery programs or enroll in a high school that they can attend until they are twenty-one. The mothers are enthusiastic about their new environment and try to get the hang of it more quickly than the previous comers. The older teens are usually more motivated than the cool families.

Finally, however, all three types of families have one common denominator: their need of relevant services.

CHAPTER TWO

Early Childhood:

First Things First

A long time ago, a little boy was born to a single mother named Amina who lived on the Arabian Peninsula. The custom of the elite at that time was to send their infants to foster mothers who lived outside the city. The foster mothers would suckle the infants for two years. Amina decided to send her baby so he "would develop a strong body and acquire the pure speech and manners of the Bedouins" (Mubārakfūrī 1995, 72). Although Amina's husband had passed away and she was a single mother, she made an effort to find a foster care family or early quality care. Amina wanted to keep her son away from the city and to expose him to a place where people spoke pure Arabic. For some reason, the foster care mother requested to keep the young boy for another two years. The boy joined his mother when he was four, and when he was six, she traveled to show him his relatives. On the way back, she died. His grandfather cared for him for two years. During those two years, the grandfather took the young boy with him to meetings and kept praising him in front of elders, telling him stories and loving him. Thus, the young child got high-quality early childhood care and an education full of storytelling, play, and love for eight years! This boy was Prophet Muhammad (peace be upon him).

Why Early Childhood Education?

"Parental knowledge of child development is positively associated with quality parent-child interactions and the likelihood of parents' engagement in practices that promote their children's healthy development" (National Academies of Sciences, Engineering, and Medicine 2016). Early childhood is the period between birth and eight years old. The quality of care and nurturing the young child gets during these crucial years will determine whether they will be successful in college or will need extra time to prepare. When young children are exposed to early quality learning and rich stimulation, they are ready for school. This readiness is vital to reading by third grade because third grade marks the end of early learning. When the child reads well by third grade, the success of post–high school and beyond is clear.

In the 1970s, a group of researchers conducted a longitudinal study about the long-term outcome of quality early care and education of young children. The research is called The Abecedarian Project, and it began with 111 children, all of whom were six weeks of age. The purpose of the study was to find out the link between quality early care and success post–high school and beyond.

The children in the program "improved cognition and educational attainment . . . [they] also improved health and health behaviors when participants were aged 21 years" (Muennig et al. 2011). This study proves that high-quality early learning has more benefits than academics.

The researchers created a special child development center for 6 weeks to 5 years, providing the best possible quality environment. After the children started school, they received a follow-up test until they were twenty-one years old. These children maintained their grade level and were successful in college and life. As we can see from this study, high-quality early learning pays off, and everyone benefits from it. Parents are happy, children receive quality care and education, more remedial and intervention programs are not needed, and above all, there is no delinquent behavior, which means no juveniles going to prison.

Your knowledge and selection of quality care and nurturing centers are what your child needs. The brains of young children develop rapidly during the first five years of life! In addition to their brains, their bodies grow as well. During this period, it is essential that we—as parents, caregivers, and educators—be attentive and provide the best high-quality early care and education for young children. During these first years, it is essential to pay close attention to several activities and periods, because they aid the linguistic, literary, cognitive, and physical development of a young child. These are the first two years, sensitive periods, storytelling, and play.

The First Two Years of a Child's Life (Prenatal and Breastfeeding)

Early care starts when the mother becomes pregnant, and as you know, the rules of Islam take measures to care for both the mother and the unborn baby. When the mother is pregnant, she should eat healthfully and take her prenatal vitamins to allow for optimal growth of the fetus, or unborn child. Due to a lack of understanding of the healthcare system and cultural practices, prenatal care among Somali women is poor.

Somali mothers avoid visiting the doctor for the first few weeks, because according to them it is not a big deal. The community is okay with this, even if the mother is not eating food or, in the worst-case scenario, becomes bedridden. A time comes when the mother feels too dizzy due to malnutrition or dehydration and calls the emergency room or shows up in Urgent Care. Next she gets only fluids, and the doctor finds out she is pregnant and prescribes prenatal vitamins. The mother goes home, throws the prenatal vitamins in the garbage, and on her next visit tells the doctor everything is well and she is taking her vitamins! I remember asking some of my friends, "Why are you throwing away the vitamins? They are good for you and the baby."

The answer I get is, "Because it is the size of a bean and makes me more sick."

Most young children in the Somali community are not breastfed long enough due to pregnancy or milk reduction caused by work or school. The working mothers are also encouraged to continue nursing their babies if they want. This is one of their rights, and they can talk to their employer. We have tools to preserve the mother's milk even if the baby is not near. She can do the same at school during her breaks so the production of milk will not be interrupted.

Somali women do not practice self-care, and that has caused multiple and complicated health issues, including depression. First, the mother does not get good prenatal care; second, after she delivers the baby she does not have a plan to space children to allow for healing and for nurturing of the baby. Six weeks after the delivery, the doctor starts the discussion of birth control methods and the mother is hesitant to say anything confidently, so she tells the doctor that she will come back later with her decision. Culturally, birth control is viewed as a foreign idea and is rejected. So, the mother becomes pregnant with another baby in two months, and she becomes sick again, and it goes on and on!

People assume birth control is a means to reduce children from the family. In fact, during the time of Prophet Muhammad (peace be upon him), people used natural birth control and he did not say anything. The difference is that now we have modern and different methods to choose from.

When mothers get good prenatal care and breastfeed their babies the recommended two-year period, they can stop birth control; when the next baby arrives, the older one is almost three years of age!

During the first two years, young children develop a secure attachment to their caregivers and parents. They are also vulnerable to diseases at this time. Thus, Islam highly recommends breastfeeding during this period to make the attachment successful. Allah tells us in the Qur'an: "Mothers may breastfeed their children two complete years for whoever wishes to complete the nursing [period]" (Qur'an 2:233).

This attachment is also what enables young children to trust adults later in life. Additionally, breastfeeding provides young children the right nutrition they need to help them develop their immune system, which helps them fight diseases. Therefore, breastfeeding during the first two years is highly recommended.

Islam makes a secure connection between early years and senior years when it comes to caring. This concept is fundamental to understanding Somali culture and its approach to parenting. Allah tells us in the Qur'an: "And We have enjoined upon man, to his parents, good treatment. His mother carried him with hardship and gave birth to him with hardship, and his gestation and weaning [period] is thirty months." (Qur'an 46:15). Premature infants need more time for breastfeeding than full-term infants. This verse explains the period of gestation and weaning, which is thirty months. For example, if the infant is born in the seventh month, we subtract six months from thirty months, which results in a period of twenty-four months.

The gestation period is when the baby is growing inside the mother's womb. If the baby is born in seven months, the baby is preterm; if the baby is born in nine months, the baby is full-term. Weaning happens when the mother begins to stop breastfeeding her baby. Although the mother's milk is a meal itself, there is a period to stop or wean off. Overall, gestation and weaning will not proceed after two years. "The American Academy of Pediatrics reaffirms its recommendation of exclusive breastfeeding for about six months, followed by continued breastfeeding as complementary foods are introduced, with continuation of breastfeeding for 1 year or longer" (The American Academy of Pediatrics 2012). As we can see, both the Qur'an and the research are on the same page when it comes to breastfeeding recommendations and its benefits.

Breastfeeding results in a strong attachment, and also "provides essential nutrition . . . some protection against common childhood infections and better survival during a baby's first year" (What are the Benefits of Breastfeeding?). Skin-to-skin contact that happens between mothers and babies has endless psychological advantages for babies, especially preterm babies. The mother's milk acts as an injection against diseases and boosts the immune system, which also helps the baby later in life. In addition to the survival and immunity boost, the consistency of the mother's milk changes to satisfy the nutritional needs of the baby's body. For example, you will notice that in the first few days, the milk is a yellowish color. This yellowish milk is called colostrum, and it is high in protein and vitamins as well as antibodies. In addition to the benefits mentioned, there are also many other benefits of breastfeeding as well. The point is, the first two years are a very crucial and sensitive period. There are many things the young child learns during this time, and no parent wants to miss these golden moments!

Sensitive Periods

Sensitive periods are like opportunities that knock on the door for babies. As parents and caregivers, we are the ones who can open that door for the baby. "The development of the system of speech sounds, or phonology, seems to be particularly susceptible to timing, which has led to hypotheses of a sensitive . . . period for the acquisition of this domain of language" (Norrman and Bylund 2016). Young children develop their language skills before they even say a word. Comprehending the sounds of words and saying them well happen because of the sensitive period. During these sensitive periods, it is important for children to have stimulation. Eighty-five percent of the brain develops before the age of five. Therefore, the mental connections children make during their early years are important. So, if there are no stimuli in their environment, they will not be able to make such connections easily later in their lives. Read stories to your baby and talk to them as early as six months so you do not miss this language acquisition time. The sensitive period is all about knowing what young children need and when. This early start is vital for young children because it helps them succeed in high school, college, and beyond!

Cognitive Development

The time the mother or the caregiver spends feeding and cuddling the young child is not insignificant. These interactions result in the young child's cognitive development. We saw that the Qur'an tells us that breastfeeding is good. Our Prophet Muhammad (peace be upon him) had high-quality early care and education and was raised by a single mother.

Insisting that we need early care centers that offer a cultural environment to our children is not going to solve the lack of quality education we already have. The reality is that these children need expert individuals who respect and communicate with parents, in addition to knowing principles of child development! I do not care what background the provider has; as a parent, I have the responsibility of looking for the best high-quality education and care for my children. Once I find that, the next task is to connect with the teachers, inspect the environment, drop in the center without an appointment, and question their daily planned activities and assessments.

To get quality early care and education programs for your children, think of three things: making the public library your friend, taking your child to early screening, and increasing your knowledge base of how children grow and develop.

Your local library is your first gateway of information, particularly early childhood education. You can ask library staff what early care services are available in your area, what books are recommended for your young one, and the schedule of the story times they do. Early screening is another amazing way to find out even more information about young early care and education centers. Contact your local school district to find out about their early childhood family education programs and when and where they do early screening. Early screening is for three-year-old children, and it helps you to know whether your child is growing well.

In addition to the early screening and taking advantage of your local library's offering, you have to equip yourself with knowledge about how children grow and learn. There is a famous Somali saying: "Biyo Sacabadaada looga oon baxaa." It translates to, "You can quench your thirst by scooping water into your palms." The wisdom behind this is to be proactive and learn what you need to know instead of waiting for another person to do it for you. You can increase your knowledge base by attending parenting classes or workshops. No one is born with knowledge—everyone gains it. Start out by becoming familiar with two things while you are making your learning plan.

First, spend time and understand the Early Childhood Indicators of Progress (https://education.mn.gov/MDE/dse/early/ind/). These guidelines are a useful tool to help you understand the developmental stages that young children go through. Look at your child's age and read the corresponding page for each subject. Take advantage of home visit programs that exist in your area and ask the early childhood educator who visits you any questions that come into your mind about the growth of your child. The Help Me Grow website also has good information and resources to help you.

I recommend visiting the Minnesota Department of Education (MDE) site. You will find helpful information about early learning and several signs that indicate progress is happening.

There are some documents that are being translated into Somali, Spanish, Hmong, and other languages. The documents are to help parents understand what we need to look for when young children are between zero to three and three to five. The majority of developmental dimensions are covered, and during the early years it is not necessary to focus on one developmental stage at a time but rather to focus on the whole child. These standards were developed so parents and educators in Minnesota can detect any developmental delay while preparing young children for successful lifelong learning!

Second, look out for Parent Aware signs on the walls and website of the early childcare center or daycare where you are trying to enroll your child. This is the number-one indication that the center is using best practices. You can even ask about the curriculum they are using, scan the environment, and see how they are welcoming parents. More information can be found on the Parent Aware website (http://parentaware.org/).

This knowledge is going to help you do your parenting duty very well and without stress. When you are working, no matter what degree you have, you will have some basic training in the setting you will work in, and there will be professional development workshops that you will be attending. The main reason for professional development is to help us enhance our performance and stay up to date in our field. Parenting is the same thing; you need to have an ongoing professional development. Plan this by putting it on your calendar that each month you will attend a parenting workshop or do self-study, however you feel most comfortable; and as always, do not forget to reach out to your network of people when things seem to be going in the wrong direction.

Back in 2013, Matthew Santori and Maureen Wagner, two graduate students from the University of Minnesota, explored the challenges and opportunities related to early child development in the Cedar-Riverside neighborhood (2013). In a meeting including parents who lived in the neighborhood, the graduate students asked questions relating to child care practices. I was one of the parents who advocated for high-quality early childhood programs. I had been using family, friend, and neighbor (FFN) care, so the meeting became a turning point for me! One main reason that parents always look for someone they know is that they are missing the support system and the extended family they had back home! For this reason, you will find, "parents usually have personal relationships with these caregivers, and therefore trust them to provide quality, culturally-appropriate care to their children" (Early Childhood Development). As a parent, culture matters to me, but I believe early childhood caregivers should also know how young children develop and grow.

According to the Center on the Developing Child at Harvard University, there are five steps to building the brain of a young child (Center on the Developing Child). The young child won't go through these steps if the caregiver is not a responsive adult. These actions occur with the "serve and return" parenting style, which is close to the "authoritative" parenting style. The difference is you—the parent, caregiver, and educator—need to find an opportunity to see what the child is interested in and then show your appreciation and return by saying something about whatever caught their attention.

So, the child is the leader, and you are the facilitator. Serve and return is an interactive method of nurturing young children. Using this method offers two advantages: first, it fosters brain growth and enhances the way your child approaches learning. Second, it fosters positive parenting and teaches parents the scaffolding method of teaching.

For example, a child picks up some Legos and starts putting them together. The parent looks and says, "Wow, what are you building?"

The child responds, "A house."

Then the parent says, "That looks amazing! Is that blue piece going to be the door of the house?"

In these interactive conversations, the child is learning, and the parent is responsive while scaffolding the learning experiences of the young child. Scaffolding is a teaching strategy developed by the psychologist Lev Vygotsky that requires you to know the zone of proximal development (ZPD), which is the distance between what children can do by themselves and the next level of learning that they can be helped to achieve with competent assistance.

Rich and stimulating interactions between the child and the caregiver/parents ensure quality care. Parents can do this with their children from babbling babies to talking toddlers!

Here are the steps to help parents implement the serve and return technique:

1. Notice the serve and share the child's focus of attention.
2. Return the serve by supporting and encouraging.
3. Give it a name!
4. Take turns . . . and wait. Keep the interaction going back and forth.
5. Practice endings and beginnings.

Step 1: Notice the serve and share the child's focus of attention.

First, you need to figure out and focus on what the child is doing or noticing. That is the "serve." It requires parents to be like detectives all the time and catch a moment when their child initiates action or discussion about the things that caught his attention—like saying, "Look at that BIRD"—and turning that into a learning opportunity.

Step 2: Return the serve by supporting and encouraging.

This is the time when your feedback nurtures and the neurons start firing up! Your child is waiting for you to show the same excitement he expressed when he saw the bird. You can say something like, "Wow, that bird was flying so fast!" Support and encourage your child by asking if they would like to see more birds and take pictures, or plan a field trip to the nature center.

Step 3: Give it a name!

This step gives your child confidence and expands his vocabulary. "The bird was a blue-throated hummingbird."

Step 4: Take turns . . . and wait. Keep the interaction going back and forth.

The real interaction between you and your child starts right now! Your job is to follow your child's lead and be responsive to his needs. Give him time to process the information while keeping eye contact with him and showing positive facial affirmation. Use the scaffolding teaching strategy when needed as you and your child think aloud in this stage.

Step 5: Practice endings and beginnings.

This concludes the present activity session. Depending on the interest of your child, you can either start another session or end and take a break. You just have to use the right words so they know what's expected of them. You will know when your child is beginning to lose interest in the current activity, is tired, and needs a break.

You and your child explored a few steps that nurture the brain and establish relationships. These interactions will also sharpen your positive or authoritative parenting skills while enhancing your child's cognitive abilities.

My point is, if someone who shares your culture is with your young child and all they do is feed the baby, put them to sleep, and make them sit in front of the TV until you come back, that is a waste of time!! No brain stimulation is happening since the adult is not interacting with the young child. Remember, about 85 percent of brain development occurs before the age of five, and if no connections happen, their brain will go through synaptic pruning.

John Piaget is best known for his theory of cognitive development. Two of the four cognitive stages—sensorimotor and preoperational—occur during the early childhood years. The first stage happens from birth to two years and the second from two to seven years. According to Piaget, young children are learning about the world around them. For example, in the second stage, "children . . . tend to be egocentric and struggle to see things from the perspective of others" (Cherry 2015). For example, telling your child under seven years old not to touch that toy or they will face the consequences of beating and punishment is unfair because the child does not understand abstract concepts. Remember, the hadith tells us to start instructing at the age of seven.

Starting to teach children at the age of seven does

not mean before seven they are not smart, but they are unable to follow two- to three-step directions to do tasks. Exposing children to high-quality programs and activities during their early years will prepare them to learn after seven years of age. Logically, when we start nurturing our children at an early age, they are tuned to what we are saying and there will be fewer behavior problems. However, if we start punishing and beating them during the early childhood years, they will become stubborn-headed and will not care much about values. They will do things mostly because they do not want to get hit. So, beating does not have any benefits, and it suppresses the intrinsic motivation to learn, listen, and have fun!

Virtues of Storytelling & the Somali Tradition

The Somali culture has a strong oral tradition. Somalia is called the "Nation of Poets" because Somalis share and exchange ideas through poems, stories, and memorized speeches. Sometimes, they do chores and solve problems while chanting poems. Somalia did not have a written language until 1972, so, at a very young age, children listen to countless stories told by family members. "Sheeko, Sheeko, Sheeko Hariiro," which translates to, "A story, a story, it is story time," is used to start a story, similarly to "Once upon a time." I remember listening to stories told by my parents, aunts, uncles, and grandmothers.

So, young children learn from lots of stories that have moral lessons. Some of the famous stories in Somali literature are *Dhegdheer*, *Will Waal*, *Egal Shidad*, and *The*

Lion's Share. These books are available here in Minnesota as paperbacks and as ebooks.

Parents, you can tell your young children oral stories in your own language and ask them questions. It doesn't matter if you do not know English. In fact, research tells us that children who know another language do better in schools. Language exposure involves speaking to young children, which perfectly matches the practices of Somali mothers! If you listen to a mother who is putting a baby to sleep, you will hear the most beautiful lullaby ever!

Some benefits of storytelling include increasing vocabulary, teaching literacy and social skills, expanding imagination, and helping children understand concepts in simple words. Visualization and story sequencing are two literacy skills children acquire through storytelling. The ability to tell what happened, when, and who did certain actions in the story is a strong indication that the child learned sequencing skills. This skill will further enhance comprehension skills when the child reads by himself. By reading to your child every day, you are cultivating an avid reader.

Oral stories also expand children's imagination and vocabulary. Each time you read a book to your child, they learn new words. Folktales and fairytales nurture their cognitive ability and help them imagine the impossible. Finally, social skills such as interacting with others, taking turns when speaking, respecting others' opinions, and learning the norms of society are accomplished during story times. Start your family story time if you have not already. Gather some famous folktales, fables, and cultural stories that you memorized and want to pass on to your child!

The Importance of Play During the Early Years

During my work at the Cedar Riverside Community School, I heard a lot of stories from concerned parents regarding children and play. I do not blame those parents for being suspicious about play. I have to confess that, before studying child development, I was one of the parents that did not think play had value at all. As Somali parents, we are serious when it comes to education thanks to our parents, who imparted this sense and love of education! Play was an integral part of our day back home, but it was just play instead of bothering adults. We had open areas to run around, chase each other, and play hide-and-seek and other games. I remember my mother used to buy me small, clay kitchen utensil sets. My friends and I used to take pieces of onion, tomatoes, and spices and actually cook them over a fire and taste the sauce! Little did we know that was nurturing our brains. So, it's the same here, except that play is structured and enhanced to ensure safety!

I knew very little about child development when I was enrolling my daughter in kindergarten. I exposed her to high-quality opportunities at an early age, and she became a reader at the age of five! Before I started working at Cedar Riverside, I even asked my daughter's kindergarten teacher to give her more homework! However, playing was not on my agenda. Some of the stories I hear from parents with kids in kindergarten say that children play all the time and the teachers do not teach anything.

Play and fun are vital for children, and there has been a lot of research done to prove it. Yet, the lack of play is apparent, especially in our small apartments and spaces for children. While children are playing, their brains develop and make lots of connections. These connections will help them later in life. Developmentally appropriate programs and environments are a must, and educators carefully select the equipment we see in schools and libraries. Therefore, it is essential to have basic knowledge of how children develop and learn. You can visit libraries or observe early learning centers and daycares to get an idea. Usually most of the furniture, toys, and setup of the area are age appropriate. Also visit stores that sell educational materials, like Lakeshore Learning, and tell them the age you are shopping for. If you look at the back or side of toys or furniture, you will find the appropriate age for that item written on it.

The dramatic play area is one thing that I would like parents to pay attention to whenever they visit early learning centers, schools, libraries, or museums. The pretend play area has appliances that are similar to our home appliances but in smaller sizes. Examples include kitchenware and utensils, doctor equipment, and fake produce like apples. Have you seen children in grocery stores with better behavior than their peers? It is likely that their parents have utilized play to instill social norms while entertaining them.

Local public libraries and children's museums are where you will find spaces dedicated to playing. They are available for you and your child anytime, without the need for registration or the concern of being put on a waiting list. The Minnesota Children's Museum is a place you and your children can visit. The Children's Museum charges a fee, but it's a small price to pay for how much it will benefit your child. Public libraries have a space designed for play, early learning, and literacy programs. Visit one of your local libraries and ask a librarian about the resources you can use to nurture your young children.

We cannot talk about all the benefits that play offers to young children, but we can provide some basic knowledge about play so you can learn more and explore it with your children!

Teach Your Children to Pray When They Are Seven Years Old

The above heading is a hadith that tells us about the concept of early childhood and how we approach it. Prophet Muhammad (peace be upon him) said: "Command your children to pray when they become seven years old, and beat them to it when they become ten years old . . ." (Sunan Abi Dawud).

The early childhood years start from birth and continue until the child is eight years old! That is until the child is in grade three. So, according to this hadith, the real education and teaching start in grade three. Many folks take the second part of the hadith as evidence to beat children when they are teaching them, forgetting their responsibility on the first part. The next chapter elaborates more on the second part of this hadith.

The Islamic approach to parenting is that parents have the responsibility of caring for and raising their children, and children are expected to be kind and obey their parents. Parents are accountable if they fail to do this task of parenting. In Islam, upbringing and education are at the center.

Exposing young children to high-quality early learning opportunities and surrounding them with nurturing and responsive caregivers will result in the child being a responsible individual by age ten. So, please do not hit children if they do not perform well or do not follow directions. Rather, guide them. We guide children's actions and behaviors by showing, explaining, reminding, and redirecting them (SERR). Show them how you want them to do things or act by demonstrating this behavior and being a role model for them. For example, if you want them to read books, grab a book and read in front of them. When you want them to understand certain rules or directions, explain according to their level of understanding. This can include following family rules, doing tasks, or learning concepts. Finally, keep in mind that children are children and need reminders and strategies to bring them back on track. Regardless of their age, children will get off track, and it is our duty as educators and parents to remind and redirect them to what they have to do. Redirecting means distracting from the activity that distracted them and bringing them back to their task. So, remember, to show, explain, remind, and redirect, or SERR!

Children are undergoing lots of changes during their early years. Physical development is one, and active play helps to build large muscles. However, that is not the only change that is happening. Cognitive development is a significant change that occurs in children too!

Children with Special Needs

I acknowledge that there are children who need special instructions, and I am here to share a story with you about a little girl who fell ill around her first birthday.

The little girl's name was Helen Keller. She was just starting to say words; the first word her parents heard was "water." She fell ill and became blind and deaf, her behavior turning wild, which frustrated her parents. Her parents wanted her to get an education, so they hired a teacher, Anne Sullivan, who was trained in a school for the blind and also had a vision problem herself.

While Sullivan was trying to observe the six-year-old little girl, "the child knocked out one of Sullivan's front teeth!" (Papalia, 144). One day, Sullivan was walking around a garden with Helen and stopped by a water pump. Sullivan pumped the water and used sign language to say "water" to Helen. Helen put her hand under the water, stopped, and started saying sounding out the letter "w"! Sullivan repeated "water," and Helen made a mental connection to the current feeling of water and said "water."

From this story, we learn the importance of early experience and exposure to a nurturing environment. We, as Somali parents, too frequently confine our young ones when they are at home, at daycare, or outside in strollers. Young children need to use their senses at a very early age. Let them splash water, break cups, and mix the pizza dough with you. Birth to two years is a time of sensorimotor skill development. Also take advantage of early childhood screening services offered at your local districts. Diagnosing problems early is always better than discovering them at a later time when the child is already in kindergarten or first grade.

Learning to Read

Teaching young children how to read may seem difficult, but with some basic knowledge and effort, you can create an avid reader!

"Reading aloud from children's literature and rich and focused instruction on sophisticated words enhances children's vocabulary" (Hill & Launder, 2010). The child may not be speaking yet, but young children listen and process the sounds of words, and once they start talking, they say things the right way due to the early exposure. Reading aloud is very close to storytelling, and children benefit from both.

Reading aloud teaches print awareness, left-to-right reading, book flipping, and book care. As parents, cultivating an avid reader has long-lasting benefits. You will not need to worry more about homework and tutoring, since every subject requires reading and comprehension. Make sure to expose your child to different genres. I have seen many parents tell their children not to take certain books because they believe they don't have benefits. I would say, do not limit your child's imagination.

Children have different interests. For example, some are interested in bugs, dinosaurs, cars, or trains. Find out what they are interested in and let them read the books they like. "Libraries are full of books new and old that will appeal to nearly every kind of child" (Dolch, 1948). Take your children to the libraries and encourage them to check out books. For example, if you want your children to have books to enhance their reading, go the leveled reading section, take two books, and let your children check out a few books about things that interest them. A win-win situation!

In addition to keeping up with books and storytelling, I will share a few tips to make your child a good reader. Make sure you don't overload your child with many questions about the story or check on the level of vocabulary gained. These will come naturally. So, first introduce the alphabet, sight words, and three-letter words.

The Alphabet

Around three years of age, your child is ready to learn to read, and they will need knowledge of the alphabet. You can sing the alphabet, read books about the alphabet, and have posters with the alphabet. I, personally, purchased a carpet with the alphabet and used to jump on the letters as I said them and then let my child do the same. You can also do this with a giant poster and point to the letters as you say them. Listening to the ABC song together is also a great way to memorize the alphabet.

Sight Words

Sight words are words that do not follow spelling rules, so you can read the words only by recognizing them. Also known as Dolch words, sight words were compiled by Edward William Dolch in 1948. They are the most frequently encountered words in children's books (such as those by Dr. Seuss), and there are 220 of them. According to Dolch (1948), there are also 95 nouns which are not part of the basic sight words. Young children learn these words visually from story books based on sight words, and there is a recommended order that they should memorize them in.

One thing to remember as a parent is, "A too early start results in dislike and in slow progress instead of rapid progress" (Dolch 1948). I know many parents, including Somali parents, like to see their child reading early. We tell children to finish activities that are sometimes developmentally not appropriate. In this case, if we force young children to read without considering their attention span and development, we are actually setting them up for failure. So, reading would seem boring, and that is not what we want.

Three-Letter Words

Three-letter words are the most exciting time because the child realizes they can actually spell out words! This stage comes after mastering the alphabet. If the child is at school, you may see teachers sending some simple books that contain these three-letter words. You can also do this at home. Get some books from the library, or ask your child's teacher to recommend some. Bobby Lynn Maslen authored and founded Bob Books that help young children learn three-letter words. Ask your local library to purchase them. They are mini books that your child can read and draw in.

CHAPTER THREE

Trust & Building Relationships

Children develop and grow at different rates, and development is defined slightly differently in every society and culture. However, there are some developmental milestones that children share no matter where they live or what their background is. There are three periods of development: early childhood (0–8), middle childhood (8–12), and adolescence (12–18). The age range of these developmental stages may be different depending on the society or culture you are talking about. Sometimes the society adjusts the age when children can do certain things or when they start school.

One thing to keep in mind is that maturation differs across cultures. In Islam, children are mature by the time they reach puberty and are held accountable for their actions. Here in the United States, children are adults when they reach eighteen. Another fact is that as young adults they still need guidance, even after eighteen, because according to research, the reasoning part of the brain develops well after twenty-one.

So according to those age ranges, we have opportunities to guide, teach, instill moral character, and maintain relationships with our children as long as they are alive!

During middle childhood, we as parents have a golden opportunity to connect with our children emotionally and be responsive to their needs. For them, peer relationships, self-image, and schoolwork become important elements. For you, schoolwork, motivation, setting limits, and disciplining become important elements too. Schoolwork is going to be a major battle between you and your child. Your child is going through major changes due to puberty. One day they are happy, the next day they are sad and you do not know what happened. During middle school, you need to establish a schedule for schoolwork with the consultation of your child, and use the guiding strategy: show, explain, remind, and redirect (SERR). It is also important to act as a cheerleader for your child so the schoolwork becomes fun!

Motivation is the drive or determination to do a task. There are two types of motivation: intrinsic motivation and extrinsic motivation. When your child does schoolwork because he wants to get good grades and be successful, he has an intrinsic motivation. When your child does the work because you promised he could have his favorite snack or go to a movie, he has extrinsic motivation.

As parents and educators, we use both types of motivation. Intrinsic motivation is a seed that you must plant in your child at a young age because that is what will help them in the long term. It becomes a challenge in the teen years to rely on intrinsic motivation, so try to develop strategies. Develop certain phrases such as, "You are a wonderful mathematician," "You will be the best doctor in the world," "I believe in you," and use them. Carol Dweck talks about mindsets in her book *Mindset: The New Psychology of Success* (2016). She mainly talks about two categories of people: those who have a growth mindset and those who have a fixed mindset. Fixed-mindset people believe things cannot be changed, while growth-mindset people believe things can be changed and that we grow even when we fail.

According to Carol Dweck, labeling is detrimental to our children's development and well-being. We, Somali parents, mostly use different phrases for boys and girls, and those phrases can impact how they see the world and treat one another when they grow up. For example, we often encourage boys to try different things even if there is risk or a cost involved. On the other hand, we discourage girls from doing or trying different things. We also unconsciously react to the actions of men and women differently, not knowing our children view those reactions as lessons that they will later practice. For example, if a woman says something controversial or pledges to make change on a certain issue, we respond by saying, "What can she do? She is just a woman." But if the same thing is said by a man, we say, "Waa runtii, rag rag dhalay" (He is right, man birthed by man).

Set Limits but Listen to the Developmental Voice

Setting boundaries on what your child can and cannot do, and communicating those with your child, helps you as parent. It is very important to understand that the boundaries you're setting should be realistic and developmentally appropriate. Children have their own way of understanding depending on which developmental milestone they have reached. So, listen to their developmental needs before setting limits.

One example of developmental needs we can hear from the 8–12 age range is, "I want to enjoy my childhood, let me have fun!" We, parents, tend to set limits on everything because we want our children to be the best. Well, sometimes the child will be best when they explore and enjoy their childhood. Imagine telling your child every day to do their homework because you want them to have good grades. On weekends, you tell them to revisit their Qur'an because you want them to be Hafiz. Here we see a problem: we are imposing rules on our children without considering their ideas and input. They do not have a choice about whether they need to learn the required material or not. They also do not have a choice about doing their schoolwork. What we need here is to plan schoolwork as well as fun time. We need balance.

During middle childhood, children need attention and achievement within their peer groups. Friends become more important, and their approval is what teens are willing to make sacrifices for. If the school is a place that engages children with extracurricular activities that they are interested in, then school will be fun. If the school is not promoting activities that attract children, you have to work hard and find activities outside school so you can keep your children active and interested. Also, in the case of two parents, make sure that you are on the same page when it comes to setting limits. As friends become more important, parents have to be very aware that setting limits actually helps children develop skills that are necessary for them. More often, if one parent says no, the child experiments with a different strategy and goes to the other parent to get permission. This can cause conflict between the two parents and may also result in hostile behavior from the child toward one of the parents.

Responsiveness Builds and Restores Relationships

I remember hearing a lot from parents, "This child doesn't listen to me but listens to other people." Sometimes we, parents, say things that we think are culturally okay, but our children do not understand what we are trying to tell them. "Parental pressures on adolescents to engage in certain behaviors can be detrimental to attachment outcomes, as they may prompt to shut off feelings and thought leading to more avoidant attachment" (Ruhl, Dolan, and Buhrmester, p.3). Attachment starts in infants and continues to build as they grow up. The level of attachment depends on the quality of the relationship the child has with others around him, including his parents. When children and teens always hear harsh words from parents such as, "Do your homework," or, "You do not understand anything," they will not communicate with parents when they need something because "adolescent perceptions of parental criticism are related to more attachment avoidance and anxiety" (Ruhl, et al, p3). When these children are in school or with other adults, and the adults show them positive attitudes and approach them with kind words such as, "Honey, you do not look like you are feeling well today. Is everything okay? Let me know what I can do," that person is responding to your child more than you do; children will listen to the person who cares about them. Humans develop attachment in their early years, but attachment can start late with a caring person too.

We, Somali parents, especially mothers, are always busy with children. We prepare food for them, clean up after them, get them ready for school, and make sure they do their schoolwork. We might think we are attached to them because we are giving our time and effort, but that is not a major attachment factor when it comes to our connectedness with them. There was a study done to determine the degrees of attachment and the factors influencing them. Researchers observed mothers to see how proactive and responsive they were to their infants. "Mothers who were available all day were not responsive to or sociable with their infants, whereas some fathers who were not frequently available interacted strongly with their infants whenever they were with them" (Bowlby, 1969. p. 315). If we are with our teens and children 24/7 but do not interact with them, or are not sensitive and responsive to their needs, another adult who is responsive might steal our children's minds—and they will listen to them more than us, their parents!

In chapter 1, we overviewed different parenting styles. One of them was the authoritative parenting style which uses responsive strategy. In Western countries, no matter what country you come from, your children are going to function better with responsive style because it is used in a majority of schools. That is why you will see your child respond positively to certain people like teachers and other community members, even trusting them more than you.

Those adults that influenced your child used tools, and you can use the same tools to restore your relationship with your child. Let us talk, for example, about responsiveness. Responsiveness is responding to the needs of the child in a timely fashion. If you give a sandwich to a friend because you have an extra one, the friend may take it and say thank you with a smile! However, you may see the same friend another day, but this time she is very hungry and you know she cannot afford to get a sandwich. You run and purchase a sandwich and hand it to your friend. The latter action was responsive and will impact your friend; she will remember you for what you did for her.

It is the same way with our children. A lot of times we do not have time to even observe and analyze what our children's needs are. Back home in Somalia, the ideal family traits were for kids to look good and clean because their father had a job and their mother cooked the food and cleaned the kids and home. However, the domains of development are not only physical. Children need to develop cognitively as well as social-emotionally!

Sometimes, we mention that we are doing everything for the good of our children. We are working for our children, saving for them, cooking food for them, cleaning their clothes, and yet they are disobeying us or are not listening to us. Well, attachment has nothing to do with cleaning and cooking only. Establishing relationships requires paying attention to the individual's needs and responding.

Sometimes we ignore what they ask us for, like going to a movie or watching a favorite sport at the stadium or Target Field. Maybe it is nothing for us, but it is a big thing for them. They see things differently, they are growing up, it is their time. It is a childhood experience, and they will talk about and remember these memories when they grow up. You can find out what your children are interested in doing, or are wishing for, by having a conversation with them in a restaurant or in the car or simply listening actively to what stories they talk about among themselves.

The Long-Lasting Impact of Beating Children

In chapter 2, we presented the first part of a hadith from our Prophet Muhammad (peace be upon him), telling us to teach our children to pray salat when they are seven years old. The second part says: "And hit if they do not pray at the age of ten." We also pointed out that forgetting the first part is detrimental to the understanding of the second part. Some people take the second part of this hadith as evidence for beating children if they do not listen! Hitting children mostly happens in cultural teaching centers and in some homes where adults believe learning occurs only when you create fear in children. This is a custom and is not acceptable, just as female genital mutilation was a custom and is illegal to do anymore.

The hadith tells us to teach them to pray at the age of seven and, if they do not pray at the age of ten, beat them. The implication of the hadith is that we should not hit children—even the slightest smack—before the age of ten. We have to nurture and guide them during their early years. After we do that, chances are they won't be disrespectful when they reach ten years old. I remember a few years back when I asked a Qur'an teacher why he beats up students, and the answer did not click with me. The teacher said to me that when the angel, Jibreel, was bringing the Qur'an down, he said to Prophet Muhammad (peace be upon him), "Read!" while squeezing him tightly. When the Prophet (peace be upon him) said, "I am not one who recites," the angel said to the Prophet again, "Read!" I am open to discussing this issue, but when I thought about it deeply, it did not make any sense to me. First, you are not an angel, and second, you are dealing with a child! Above all, as we will see in chapter 5, we are beating children to make them do a task that even the parents are not able to and that is not required!

Another reason we are beating our children is because this is what we saw our trusted adults around us doing when we were children. Allah tells us in the Qur'an, "And when it is said to them, 'Follow what Allah has revealed,' they say, 'Rather, we will follow that which we found our fathers doing.' Even though their fathers understood nothing, nor were they guided?" (2:170). I am willing to further discuss this topic with any parent or teacher who cares about children and their future life. This is not an accident—the beating is a cycle that keeps on going and ruining the lives of our growing generations. Remember, as parents, we have power over our children the same way managers have power over their employees. If we do not use our power properly, we are abusing our power. These physical punishments leave scars that you cannot see most of the time, scars that will cost you your future relationship with your own children. The psychological impact will also not be beneficial to what they are learning and hearing! The only time we parents wake up and panic is when Child Protective Services becomes involved and interviews the child. They then receive different answers, which makes the case even more complicated. This is plain abuse, and doing it while claiming that we are teaching our children our culture is not the right thing. Our religion does not endorse our action, and our culture has negative aspects that we need to avoid after assessing the damage it does to us and to our children.

Anas bin Malik (RA) said, "I served the prophet—may Allah bless him and grant him peace, for ten years. He never said 'uff' to me and never said about anything I had not done, 'Why didn't you do that?' And he never said about anything I have done, 'Why did you do that?'" We can see from this hadith how Prophet Muhammad (peace be upon him) used to treat children, and isn't he our role model? Or we are bringing our own models while claiming we are Muslims?

In psychology, we learned that if you take information in while you are in a certain mood, you will retrieve that information well when you are in the same mood. This is called mood-congruent memory. Children who have been hit while trying to memorize the Qur'an may be able to recall that information more easily when they are fearful. In this case, please let us learn from the Qur'an and the science about how children learn and when. Dear parents and teachers, tell me, who of the companions of Prophet Muhammad (peace be upon him) were beaten up so they could learn the Qur'an? What we are practicing is purely an abuse cycle with no tie to our faith.

I learned the Qur'an at a young age, and my dugsi teacher was the same teacher that my mother had. I do not recall being beaten up. Maybe other factors helped me escape. However, one vivid thing I remember is, while I was playing with children near our house, all of a sudden the children ran away and hid. Of course I ran after them, and after the dugsi teacher passed us by, everything became normal.

These students are going to grow up tomorrow, and how do you want them to face you in society? Do you want them to run away from you? Or do you want them to run to you, smile, and thank you for how well you taught them valuable lessons?

Character and Resilience

We all like a child who behaves well, listens well, and is at the top of the class! We adults, including parents, sometimes forget we were once children. Character building starts at home, and we are role models for our children. We have to do what we want them to, and we have to act the way we want them to act. For example, if you want your child to respect and help people, you do it first and do it naturally. Be involved in your community, school, and dugsi, and do not criticize some teachers and praise others because of differences in culture and religion. If you want your child to be an avid reader, you go to the library, grab a book for yourself, and start reading it enthusiastically and talking about it.

Resilience is the ability to bounce back after crisis or problems. We all had problems in the past, and those thoughts sometimes haunt us and pull us back. You might think that your child will never be successful in school because he was born in a refugee camp, did not have good education and income to support him, and is now sitting with children who were in this country and had plenty of opportunities. Well, because of resilience, children are able to reach their potential with the help of adults. Never let past thinking control your present actions and future decisions. When flowers seem to be dying because they did not get enough water and nutrition, water them and give them a chance to grow—you might see flowering.

CHAPTER FOUR

Teenage Times

A youth came to Prophet Muhammad (peace be upon him) and asked permission to practice fornication, and companions tried to quiet him. Prophet Muhammad (peace be upon him) beckoned the youth over and asked him whether he would like this for his mother, then sister, then daughter. The youth answered no. Then the Prophet replied that this person was going to be someone else's sister, daughter, or mother. The moral of this story is that teens will have feelings, and they need guidance and a mentor. The only person they will share with is going to be someone they trust. Who in the community, family, and school has this level of trust that the teen can ask anything without fear?

As is clear from the above hadith, our teenagers are not able to weigh the consequences of their impulses, actions, and feelings. They will say anything that comes to their mind. However, they need an adult who is there to guide them and not judge them. We will explore some of the hot topics that come to our mind when it comes to teenagers: teaching them to treat their parents well, giving them guidance and mentorship, and helping them through an identity crisis or peer pressure. As their brains develop, more complicated internal changes take place during the adolescent period!

Brain Development and Physiological Changes

The human brain has several regions, and each region develops in its own time. When our teens act wild, we parents assume that they are going insane. We see them texting while driving and causing horrible accidents, as well as making bad decisions about drugs and engaging in delinquent behavior. As parents, we sometimes think our teens have gone mad or are disobedient (caasi waa-lideyn) but the reality is there are some forces that are acting on them that are out of their control! Little do we know that the brain responsible for decision making is not fully developed for our teens.

The part of the brain that is still developing is called the frontal lobe or the executive function. "This is the last area of the brain to mature and is thought to develop well into 20s" (Herrman, p 2). We see most parenting crises in the Somali community become apparent when children hit puberty and all the hormonal changes start to take effect. In addition to making poor decisions, teens act on their feelings. The amygdala is the feeling part of the brain and is more active in the teenage years, which is another reason why our adolescents may make big decisions in a matter of moments. Parents begin seeking solutions after they see their young child suddenly start acting like another creature. Some parents send the child to cultural classes back home, while others just hide their pain and feelings of shame about the behavior of their child.

Also, culturally, we have different ages for maturity based on the particular environment the child grows up in. For example, reaching fifteen years of age brings a sense of maturity to the minds of many Somalis. You can hear young girls telling each other, "I am not accountable until I am fifteen." They did not make this up; they heard it from adults around them, including parents. Now I have a teenager who always says, "I cannot wait till I am sixteen to drive a car." Similarly, most teens talk about being eighteen so they can move away from their parents' home and become free from restrictions now that they have reached maturity. Those wishes are constructed in the society we live in and the culture in which we grew up. We even have a famous song from a Somali singer, Hassan Adan Samatar, about when he was fifteen and started wishing to marry. In Islam, you are mature when you hit puberty. The main reason Somalis talk about fifteen is that most girls were believed to get their periods at the age of fifteen, but now we know it can happen any time after ten years. So, Somali parents expect their mature children, mostly after the age of fifteen, to be more responsible, and they like to see the results of their efforts to raise a sound child.

The work of parenting is not over in the teen years, and it actually becomes intense. As we know, "It takes a village to raise a child." First, parenting knowledge will help parents relax because they will come to know that there are some things that are out of their hands and the hands of their children, and that they are not alone in this work. Hormonal changes are like hurricanes seeking to destroy teens and the adults around them, including parents. We prepare for hurricanes and seek shelter to be safe because we know if we do not seek shelter, we might destroy our lives. Similarly, there are hormones that are working inside teenagers that we do not see but still experience through their behavior. Teens are sometimes moody, sometimes outrageous, and at other times are trying to take risks and do things that we parents do not approve of at all! For example, we see our teens are sometimes too lazy to wake up, and we get frustrated with them. We want them to go to school early and do chores more than before, and yet they seem to be getting lazier and lazier. Let us see what the hormone melatonin is doing to them.

I am sure as parents the hormones we know are the sex hormones because they are responsible for all those physical changes happening to teens. However, what we, parents, are not very familiar with is the hormone melatonin. Melatonin gets activated in the dark and helps us sleep, but in teens the release time is delayed. That is why teens do not fall asleep until midnight or after. We can try several strategies, but we have to believe that they are not acting up and are in need of our help. Neuroscientists have used brain scans to prove this, and you can find lots of resources to learn more about melatonin and changes in circadian rhythm during adolescence.

The big question we have to try to answer is, are teens getting enough sleep and how will it impact them if they don't? Mary Carskadon, an American sleep researcher, says that insufficient sleep "affects both their mood and their ability to think and their ability to perform and react" (Carskadon). I am sure we have experienced how difficult it is to wake up a middle schooler or high schooler early in the morning for school or dugsi. If you ask any parents in the world, they will share with you that they think their teen is lazy. When we do not allow teens to have enough sleep, we are adding to the problems we already have in terms of their behavior.

Another amazing thing that happens in the brain during the adolescent period is pruning and myelination. Myelination and pruning during adolescence are similar to the changes that happen during the first three years of childhood. This is a sensitive period, and it opens a window of opportunity for our teens. It is very important that parents take advantage of this process because it happens when the child is entering adulthood and the challenge of autonomy starts. You can expose your growing teen to a variety of learning opportunities and instill good manners. During this time, youth have more energy than we think. They are able to learn multiple skills because their brain is so hungry for something new!

If we ignore, or become too busy for, our children, they will still learn new things to satisfy their hungry brains. These new things may not be something we agree with or like. Using drugs and hanging out with bad friends may be options. If the environment where you live offers opportunities for youth like book clubs, swimming, and other sports, and the child had quality early childhood education, maybe things will be different. However, guidance and mentorship for your child are a must.

May Allah prevent our youth from undesired activities and guide them to those activities that will benefit themselves and society at large.

Many "problems of youth, including reckless behavior, fighting, vandalism, substance abuse, stealing, and trespass[ing]" (Herrman 4), are caused by an impulse feeling and prematurity of the executive function of the brain, the prefrontal cortex. This may seem negative, but it's a survival skill that develops at this particular time. Say you bought a house and you want to move but the construction is not over yet. The outside is so beautiful, but when you go inside you hear all the noises and banging, and even start sneezing because of the dust that is coming from the construction. Teens are this way: they grow up so quickly, and we expect them to do more than they did before, but inside of them many changes are happening.

Imagine telling our teens "Do your homework" 24/7 while they are going through all those changes. Who else is going to help if we, parents, do not take a proactive role? The educators are putting the blame on us, and the policy makers are signing grant money to combat youth behavior. Yet, the root cause of the problem is not being addressed as needed. Our children are being bombarded by extracurricular activities, so, as parents, we do not have time to wait until policy makers, educators, and community members come together. We need to use the advice of neuroscientists that are discovering these amazing changes happening inside our teens' brains. Our job for now is yes, to advocate, help whoever is doing work, but save our children before we lose them.

I would like to invite parents to watch this documentary from PBS that gives us a perfect view of teenage and parent life. Feel free to pause and take a break as

I did because it is so relevant to every parent who has a teenager (https://www.pbs.org/wgbh/frontline/film/inside-the-teenage-brain/).

When you know something is happening, at least it is not a surprise to you, and you have two options: ignore it and do not complain, or do something. We cannot eliminate the factors, but we can surely manage their impact on our teens.

Identity Crisis and Peer Pressure

We often hear about youth having identity crises, but where did this concept come from and what is identity crisis? Well, Erik Erikson coined the phrase "identity crisis" in his developmental theory to explain the transition from childhood to adulthood. However, we have to consider the environment the child is growing up in because not every teen goes through an "identity crisis." For example, in our culture, when the older child is already helping the family business after high school graduation, he is the leader of the business and has skipped the career "identity crisis." Similarly, if you tell your child that you will help with his college if he enrolls in the medical school and the child wants to be in another field, there is no opportunity or exploration happening.

Teenagers are going through changes, whether we call it exploration or crisis, but the most important thing is to provide them with the support they need in transitioning from childhood to adulthood.

We often hear our teens say, "No one can tell me what to do" or see them wearing clothes that are not culturally appropriate. Two things that are happening here are the need to stand out and be cool and the need to belong to a group. Teens are trying to be independent decision makers; they think if they obey, they are weak, and instead decide to constantly and forcefully say no. This is the same way toddlers say "No" to everything because they need to be autonomous. We call that stage the "terrible twos." Let's say we are now dealing with the "terrible teens," except that they have grown up and are walking without assistance.

On the other hand, most teens are wearing certain fashions because they are trending. If your teen does not conform, they may feel left alone and try to mingle by dressing how their peers do! Peer groups are healthy in this way. Problems arise when teens do not try to separate themselves as individuals and instead do what others do because they are striving to be accepted into the culture of their peers. "Peer group acceptance and good relationships work as protective factors against social anxiety and depression" (Ragelienė 2016). When adolescents are involved in good activities and are not harming themselves, they develop healthy habits throughout their life. Youth also need "a supportive social environment where they can freely discuss what they are and who they would like to be" (Ragelienė 2016). This can be in schools, libraries, or community centers with adult mentors and coaches who are tuned in to the betterment of the lives of youth.

Islam teaches that the older person becomes kind to the young ones and young ones respect the older ones; the relationship is reciprocal, and perfecting that relationship requires efforts from both parties. Parents have a responsibility to raise their children well. They have to care about what they eat, where they go, and what they learn. They also have to make sure that their children's learning has some character education components such as kindness, compassion, and caring. The character education, as we mentioned previously, is not accomplished only by lecturing, but showing what it means to be kind, to be compassionate, and to be a good leader. Parents, teachers, and the society have to model that.

A dysfunctional family is one where the mother cannot correct her child properly because the father does not agree with the way she is addressing the problem. The child then starts playing a game between parents, thinking he or she can get away with the mistake.

Imagine if, instead of being kind to our young children, we beat them, treat them with harshness, and speak to them with language that hurts them internally, not realizing that they are still growing up and need time to absorb and analyze concepts. We sometimes throw them HABAAR or curse them, and they never stop the behavior because, as we saw, their brain is still under construction. I am not saying the cursing is not valid, but this is how Allah willed their brains to develop.

The Somali culture of child-parent relationships that last forever is amazing. You can see this from how Somalis are connected to their families back home: some send money every month and make phone calls. So the relationship between children and parents never stops. Parenting continues and being kind to parents continues.

Generally one who has a good character will automatically be good to adults around him, let alone his own parents that become old.

Guidance and Mentorship

Mentoring is something that our youth are in need of. The word "mentor" may trigger some parents because it brings back some stories of countering violent extremism (CVE) and similar community programs that confused parents and increased the lack of trust they already had in the services available to them. However, what I am talking about is not a specific program but mentoring in general. Guidance is important in order for our youth to thrive and succeed. Who mentors your child and where you find them, is a separate issue. You as a parent will be a big partner in this effort, but know that you need someone who is knowledgeable about children and their needs and who will connect them to opportunities according to your child's interests.

There are also specific problems that our teens face that we must deal with. For instance, we are witnessing how addiction damages the lives of our youth. This is a habit they develop, and we can help them develop healthy habits instead. The brain grows addicted to what we repeat over time. Teens also have road rage, impulse reactions, and so on.

Additionally, we are isolating our youth more than ever. If for example, a youth tries to go in the masjid and wants to escape from some groups that he doesn't like, everyone in the masjid might question why he is there.

Our community centers are also indirectly welcoming certain youth and ignoring others. Who is going to work and save our youth? How about we replace those bad habits with good ones? We can help them develop skills like effective planning, healthy eating habits, a good sleeping schedule, and managing emotions. Yes, this is how they will deal with difficulties later in their lives. What our youth are lacking today are life skills. Some of those skills do not need direct teaching but modeling instead. For example, in after-school activities, we can create a project about nutrition and exercise. They can do group research. Go to a local farmers market to get those fresh veggies and fruits, create a presentation and share it with the community, or make a video to share with the community and ask them how they are planning to implement what they learned. In this activity, youth are learning management skills, healthy eating habits, and planning.

Our youth are also in need of proper guidance from those who really care about their future. Today we have two groups of youth: some on the streets and others who are extremists. One group focuses on the masjid and the other are troublemakers. In both cases, we, parents, are responsible because we are their role models, whether we accept it or deny it. We treat our boys and girls differently, and tomorrow they will repeat the same mistake. We saw at the beginning of the chapter that a youth asked Prophet Muhammad (peace be upon him) a weird question. Think about if the same youth were to ask us that question—we would have different answers if the youth were a girl or boy. In our Somali culture our reaction to the questions of this youth might be something like "Oh, he has achieved his manhood!" We would acknowledge the feelings unconsciously while still thinking the question was weird. However, if that same question came from the mouth of a girl, we would say, "Shame on you, what did you just say?" That is why before the girls even reached puberty, we stitched their private parts or performed female genital mutilation (FGM) as a protective measurement.

Islam has different solutions for the issues of youth without denying a feeling that is biological and out of peoples' hands. These issues remain, whether we try to perform unnecessary surgery on girls or ship our boys to another land thinking they will behave the way we want them to behave!

Character and self-control are skills that we need to instill in our youth as well as ourselves. Although some of our parents say when children misbehave, "They become American, they do not listen and obey!" my answer to that would be, "They are children and are still growing up, let's see what is upsetting them." Certain behaviors, like having a boyfriend or girlfriend, are big issues in our community. Well, let us be honest with ourselves, we think they are having sex, right?

We all were friends and talked to each other before we married, whether it was a marriage for love or an arranged marriage. Teenagers need this time with their significant other too, but yes, having sex before marriage is HARAM. You might say, "But the environment is an environment that is promoting sex, and we cannot control and look after our children." However, when our children are ordering pizza from restaurants and online and are asked what kinds, they are saying no pepperoni or pork product. Why? Because we instructed them straightforwardly, and they know what to do whether we are with them or not. We can do the same with sex education.

Peer pressure sometimes forces us to do bad things. In this case, our youth are more vulnerable since their frontal lobe has not developed well yet. Bad company means going down the Satan path, and Satan of course tells us to do bad things. Allah says in the Qur'an, "O you who believed, do not follow the footsteps of Satan—indeed he enjoins immorality and wrongdoing" (24:21). Two words in this verse are Munkar (wrongdoing) and Fahsha (immorality). Munkar means prohibited, dreadful, evil actions and killing of people. Fahsha is evil deeds, sins, illegal sexual intercourse, and so on. All these things are visible today in our society, and youth are the victims since adults also find themselves in these situations.

So yes, there are feelings and desires to have sex, and Islam acknowledges that. Prophet Muhammad (peace be upon him) advised youth who are able to marry and those who cannot afford marriage expenses to observe fasting. So, fasting is another way to control your desires. We do this in Ramadan. We cannot eat even the halal food to train ourselves and also develop empathy for those who cannot purchase food.

We, as Muslims, are required to pray five times a day. Prayer is a solution to problems we and our youths have if we perform it the right way and with the right intention. Remember, intentions are required and part of our faith. The Qur'an tells us, "indeed, prayer prohibits immorality and wrongdoing" (29:45). There is no room for Munkar and Fahsha, and the actions they result in, after we perform salat! We may see people praying or coming out from the mosque and doing those actions. Their prayer was not effective and they need to work on their iman.

Our faith, or iman, becomes weak, and that is why our salat is not effective and du'a might not be accepted. Yes, our faith decreases and increases according to our deeds. It is like the weather forecast: sometimes there is a low degree and sometimes there is a high degree, but in iman, we do not see the degrees physically. There are some tools that we can use to increase our iman. These tools include staying away from haram and helping people. We can volunteer in our community and encourage our youth to contribute to their community. Helping people results in gratefulness, kindness, empathy, and cooperation. Staying away from haram includes not lying to anyone, Muslim or non-Muslim, in order to obtain benefits, and lowering your gaze (no exposure to porn). We do not need to purchase halal food if we are not obtaining the money we are purchasing it with in a halal way.

If I ask, "Why did you not do what I told you a few minutes before?" to one of my teens, I get different answers depending on the personality of the child. One reacts defensively, one apologizes, and the other says, "Oh, I forgot it, do not worry, I will do it right now!"

Sometimes we think teens are lying all the time, but in reality there is something going on in their minds that is out of their control. How can we, as parents, help them past these years and give them opportunities rather than making things difficult with shouting, school suspension, juvenile time, and so on?

Now that we know what is happening to our teens, the question is what can we do to maximize those effects and help them be resilient individuals? Theodore Roosevelt said, "Do what you can, with what you have, where you are." As parents, we will do what we can with what we have and leave the rest to Allah. In the next chapter, I will share resources that are useful; please take advantage of those and customize the resources to your unique needs. Each family has different needs and so does each teen. Be careful of not letting our children help to decide what we are doing. Let them be involved with in-depth activities so that they master any skill they like to do in their free time. Our Somali teens are sometimes lacking the ability to choose their own activity. For example, almost every Somali teen girl I ask, "What are you planning to learn in college after you finish high school?" says they will be a nurse. This past summer, I interacted with a teen who was a nurse. The answer was because her mother wanted her to be a nurse.

Our teens are in need of our advice, not our control. We are also making mistakes by saying a profession is not good because our religion does not allow it. Believe me, I sometimes become speechless when parents tell me they told their child not to choose a certain major in college because of our religion. Please ask a scholar before you say anything regarding the religion!

Mentoring happens when someone who has specific knowledge helps another person to enhance their specific knowledge. Mentoring is a very important tool that most people use in life, academics, and professional settings. Our children and youth today do not have access to mentoring services due to barriers. These barriers include a lack of culturally sensitive and responsive mentor models.

In the United States, mentoring is valued, and there are several formal programs, such as 4-H, that provide mentoring to youth and children. Mentoring can also be informal and come from peers, parents, or a relative or trusted community member. Whoever becomes a mentor for your child, remember you as parents are always mentors for your child. If you can get one that is fine, but if things becomes difficult, you can be the best mentor in the world!

Mentors were not born like that. They learned; they had mentors too, and so can you. First get a mentor for yourself, maybe a mentor to help you with your parenting skills. Then, after a few workshops and connections with your school and understanding the way things are going, you will start guiding your child. You can help them decide what classes to enroll in for high school, what career they are interested in, what activities will be beneficial for that career, and so on. When things do not go the way you want, grab a close and trusted friend and ask them to mentor your child. If you get a professional mentor from the community, amazing. If not, keep the momentum, and do not wait until funds become available from the community.

CHAPTER FIVE

Education: Islamic or Secular

This chapter will provide a brief and basic overview of the American education system as well as the cultural and Islamic views of education. Through cultural understanding and the education system, we will explore required education and its goals. Somali parents value education so much that they sacrifice almost everything for the sake of educating their children. They want their children to be the best in every subject while instilling in them their cultural heritage and Islamic traditions.

Current State of Somali Education in the USA

I would like to highlight our current state of education in order to help us understand our ability as parents and see how we can move forward. Our children today are attending several educational centers, including normal schools, weekend schools, and daycare centers. Of course, we parents are the ones waking children up and driving them to those centers. Yes, as Nelson Mandela said, "Education is the most powerful weapon which you can use to change the world."

In chapter 2, we discussed the importance of early childhood education and how some periods are golden opportunities for young children! Today our children are operating 24/7 every week like a machine. On weekdays they go to school, and after school they go to a homework help center or daycare center if they are younger than 12 years old. On weekends, they go to dugsi.

The cycle goes on and on, and yet parents, especially mothers, are so depressed and tired.

The story is not over yet; these children are lacking contact and close communication with their parents because they spend most of their time outside the home. The children become vulnerable to sickness due to lack of sleep and adequate nutrition. During the teenage years, stress and depression become a major thing for children, and the way to handle this is the way they see their peers handling it: look for a group to belong to and use drugs to pass the time.

Imagine if all those educational centers and mosques that the children are spending their time in were nurturing while providing educational opportunities! The story would be totally different than the current chaos we are witnessing in our children and youth.

Our love of education and good character is even forcing us to send our children back home where we think they will acquire the religious and cultural teachings that we, parents, failed to instill in them or thought they were receiving on weekends!

Overview of the American Education System

Whether your child is going to public, charter, private, or home school, there are some basic things they all share. If you pay close attention to every family in America, no matter what their background is, they have some degree of confusion as to which school is the best and what skills children need to function in the society. The struggle of education is not exclusive to Somali parents, but some parents have learned how to manage and prioritize education so they can have some type of control over what their children are learning and who is teaching them!

I remember back in 2001, when I worked for Minneapolis Public Schools as a bilingual aid, there were a lot of problems happening on the bus. The principal of the school I was working for at the time requested that I ride the bus with the students from Cedar Riverside and watch them to reduce issues. It worked—we had fewer complaints from parents, and children reached the school without fighting.

Today, the problems that were occurring on the bus have expanded into classrooms, and as a result of that, the majority of teachers are not actually teaching students but are busy dealing with behavior issues! Students are getting fewer teaching hours and are told to take tests that they are not ready for. When the results of the test come back and parents see that the student performed lower than the average, parents get frustrated and get a tutor so the child catches up with their grade level. So, we see here, teachers, students, and parents are all tired and frustrated, and communication is not smooth.

You may ask, then, what type of school is good, since K–12 education is compulsory and the students are getting fewer hours of teaching? Well, first, let's see how the schooling is divided.

"Education is the passport to the future, for tomorrow belongs to those who prepare for it today," Malcolm X said. In order to prepare your children for tomorrow, you have to be able to navigate the K–12 education system. The majority of Somali parents, especially mothers, are busy with the education of their children. However, lack of understanding of the system and the language barrier are getting in the way of parents fully engaging with the school. There are several minor things that get ignored, and when those accumulate they are difficult to reverse. These things include how the grades function and what children are learning in each grade, as well as how often you need to visit the school and engage with the administration and teachers.

K–12 Education

In the United States kindergarten is not required, but that does not mean you should not enroll your child. Grades 1–5 are called elementary school, grades 6–8 are called middle school, and grades 9–12 are called high school. In high school, each year has a name. Grade nine is called "freshman," grade ten is called "sophomore," grade eleven is called "junior," and grade twelve is called "senior." Students are required to have state tests starting in grade three. Before grade three, they will have tests administered by teachers. There are some years that the students' state test will include some extra subjects. For example, I used to run an afterschool program when I worked at Cedar Riverside Community School. I used to tell parents that if their children are in grades five or eight, they have to practice science in addition to language arts and mathematics. Finally, know that early childhood is not required but is highly recommended. When children are three years old, they can be enrolled in a preschool program. Try to find one that is a high-quality program with knowledgeable staff.

Semester or Quarterly Tests

Depending on the school they are enrolled in, your children will be taking tests every three to four months, and teachers will communicate this through parent-teacher conferences and hand you a progress report card. The progress report card says a lot about your child's progress. You can find the dates your school is going to have conferences on the school calendar, which is available either in the school office or on the school website. If you are homeschooling your child, all the progress reports and calendars are something that you as a parent will be required to make and keep on track. This will not be true if you enrolled your child in an online school. It is similar to homeschooling because you have to be responsible and make sure the child finished the required daily assignments, but you will have training on how to access the calendar and the progress report online.

As a parent, understanding the school system and how often children are tested is going to make your parenting process easier. You will develop a strong connection to your child, and when you go to parent-teacher conferences, you can discuss with your child whether he wants to join the conference or has any questions. Your child will also have inner confidence when he sees that you are concerned about his school activities. Language may be a barrier, but believe me, when you know what you are doing in your own language, finding a translator is easier, and you will also strengthen your language and communication skills since you will be asking questions back and forth in the school office and with the teachers.

K–12 education is the foundation of all higher education and the future that you want for your child. Be involved early, ask more questions, and you will find yourself learning, because the more you understand the education system, the more your motivation to learn becomes higher.

State Tests and Curriculum

Let's focus on Common Core and state standards. Schools use different curriculum materials to meet the state standards. For example, the state of Minnesota has K–12 Standards (www.education.mn.gov/MDE/dse/stds/) that are available on the education website. The yearly state test of Minnesota is called the Minnesota Comprehensive Assessments (MCA). You will find this information, and how to help your child prepare, on the Minnesota Department of Education Website. There is also something called Common Core (http://www.corestandards.org/read-the-standards/) that most states follow. These standards are intended to be a guide, and the curriculum is designed from them. When you read, for example, the Minnesota K–12 Academic Standards in English Language Arts, you will find that each grade level has to master certain skills before starting the next skill. However, when you see the reality of a typical school, students are not acquiring these skills due to several factors but will still be tested on them. Most teachers do not have enough time for every child in the classroom. Another factor is that your child may have joined the class late or may be new to the country. Whatever the factor is, making sure that your child gets quality early education and care and taking them to libraries and learning centers will make your child academically successful. So, some schools have a strong curriculum and superb staff—some benefits of sending your child to such schools include smart students and acceptance to prestigious colleges and universities!

Our children are not getting quality early learning, and they perform lower on state tests and struggle in middle school. Similarly, when our children start high school, they are unable to catch up because they missed several concepts and core subjects in middle school. So, Somali parents spend a lot of money and effort in order to avoid dropouts and low performance in high school because it is a big deal. The parents get relief when their child graduates, and yes, they brag that their child is going to college or university to become a doctor, nurse, or lawyer.

The Homeschooling Process

When I began homeschooling my children a few years ago, I was nervous and not sure I was always teaching the right things. Later on, I figured out that I was over-teaching! At first, I had to do some processes quickly after I pulled my child from second grade due to dissatisfaction. I contacted my district, told them my intention to homeschool my child, and got the forms and filled them out. Then I had to purchase the curriculum and plan my year.

After the first year of doing everything by myself, I switched to an online charter school, and my role as a parent became a Learning Coach. They sent me the curriculum materials, and my children had their own homeroom teacher, math teacher, science teacher, and so on. It is similar to regular school except you are in your house and the teachers are in their offices, but you can meet them any time you want.

In Minnesota, parents have the power to homeschool their children if they want. This Minnesota statute can be found at www.revisor.mn.gov/statutes/?id=120b.31. Look for subdivision 4a for information on homeschooling. Please find the statute of your state if you live outside of Minnesota. Also visit this site for tools and information for parents who want to homeschool their children. The site also offers alternatives to homeschooling.

Higher Education

Higher education includes colleges and universities. Community, or technical, colleges are two years. If the student finishes a two-year college, he will have an associate's degree. In the first two years of college, students can finish requirements or learn specific things like computer skills or medical assistance to get a startup job.

After college, your child can go to a four-year university as an undergraduate student and earn a bachelor's degree. If the student decides to continue in higher education, the student can enroll in a graduate school and earn a master's degree or even a PhD.

In college, most Somali students are eligible for financial aid but don't realize the aid has a limit. If parents did not take charge of their child's education and the child is not ready for college, two things are going to happen in college:

1)   Your child will start acting out, hang out with bad friends, try drugs, or join extremist groups.

2)   Your child will be taking basic classes for too long at what should have been a two-year college, and the financial aid for the four-year period will finish by the time your child finally transfers to a four-year university.

Some of you may already be witnessing such cases and asking yourselves, "Why it is taking so many years to complete general education in college?" Well, understanding a few things about the education system, especially the portion you as a parent need to know to help your child, will prevent later disappointments. The best practice to follow is asking questions early in your navigation of the education system. The strategy that personally worked for me was thinking at the top level. Start planning college or university first, and then high school, middle school, elementary school, and early learning. Let's say you want to earn your high school diploma or GED. The first thing you have in mind is the big goal: I want to get my GED so I can go to college. Okay, now you will go enroll in ESL class. The teachers tell you that you will be placed in a certain level, and for example, when you reach level five or six, you can start actual preparation for the GED. You will have a plan, and if you stick to it, one day you will get your GED.

Now, suppose you want your child to go to college and graduate on time without losing time, money, and your precious energy! Plan right now, be involved and engaged in your child's school, know what each grade needs to learn, and do not wait for a teacher or counselor to direct your child. Take charge. Become familiar with the early learning standards, Common Core, and the Minnesota state (or your state) colleges' and universities' websites.

While keeping in mind the big picture of sending your child to university, I would also like you to think smarter and know shorter ways of helping your child reach their goals. The postsecondary enrollment option (PSEO) is one of the ways you or your child can quickly earn college degrees for free if you live in Minnesota or Ohio.

PSEO is an opportunity for your child, and you have to think about this during middle school to get the best results. I learned this the hard way. Most of us Somali parents think of college when our children start high school, but the reality is that preparing early is ideal. Colleges use the results of the eighth grade Minnesota Comprehensive Assessments (MCA) test to allow the student to start PSEO in tenth grade. So, you must know how many opportunities you as parents have to navigate and try for your child. Mostly, PSEO is common for students to start in eleventh or twelfth grade, but if you want your child to start in tenth grade, the preparation usually starts in middle school, the same way middle school success starts in the early learning periods.

Education and the Islamic Traditions

Islam values education and encourages an individual's pursuit of it. In fact, the first few verses that Allah revealed to Prophet Muhammad (peace be upon him) emphasize the importance of acquiring knowledge. We Somalis are often in a state of confusion when it comes to sending our children to an Islamic school or another school. We are mixing up the spiritual and moral knowledge we are obliged to know, like praying and fasting, in order to perform our religious duties with the rest of our education.

Allah said in the Qur'an, "Recite in the name of your Lord who created" (96:1). This very first verse of the Qur'an is about recitation of the Qur'an and learning about essential knowledge of worshiping Allah. The third through the fifth verses of the same Surah are about acquiring the knowledge that we need to function in this world. Allah says, "Recite, and your Lord is the most Generous—Who taught by the pen—Taught man that which he knew not" (96:3-5). The Qur'an tells us that we, humans, learn by reading and writing. The first verse that said, "Recite," emphasizes recitation of the Qur'an, and the third verse is about reading. Learning to read comes before writing and is our obligation. Allah said in the fourth verse, "Who taught by the pen," and this is about learning to write. One may ask what we read and write as Muslims, and many people misunderstand the whole concept of learning and acquiring knowledge in Islam. The fifth verse says, "Taught man that which he knew not." This is the new knowledge that we humans are acquiring from day to day, whether it is getting the next degree, discovering new technology, or participating in professional development to help us enhance our performance.

The Qur'an points out that education is very important and a necessary tool to have, since the very society we live in demands specific education to acquire a career. Without knowledge we would not know how to pray, and without knowledge we would not know what a water molecule is made up of. Islam specifically points out three things: reading, writing, and acquiring other knowledge and skills. Do we learn reading and writing, get some skills, and then finish? No, in Islam there is some required education depending on the situation and setting, and the rest becomes optional. Similarly, the Department of Education has some requirements and goals for education. In other words, prioritization is needed in every society you live in!

First, know that whether you are in Somalia or in the diaspora, in Islam you must have some basic knowledge as a Muslim and understand what is required and when it is required. The required education is called Fard Al-Ayn, obligatory knowledge. You're also required to pass on this education to your children. One example of this obligatory knowledge is called Ibaadaat, worshiping acts.

In Ibaadaat, you have to know the rules and regulations of the five daily prayers, which are one of the five pillars of Islam.

Second, every state or country you live in has educational requirements. For example, in Minnesota, children in grades one through twelve are required to attend school. Then, to make sure that the child is on track, they take the Minnesota Comprehensive Assessments (MCA) in grades three through twelve. Remember that there is no such thing as secular education. Education is education, and Islam obligates you to learn how to read, write, and also acquire any new technology and skills necessary for you to function in the society you live in!

Weekend Learning or Dugsi

Weekend school is a school where Muslims or Somali children go to study Quran. The schools we have here in Minnesota run Saturdays and Sundays, but in some parts of the country they are just run on Sundays to give children at least one day of quality family, friends, and entertainment.

For the Qur'an and Arabic, see the archive site (https://archive.org/details/ChildrensIslamicEducatio nalSeries-IslamicStudies-Grades01To12) and use what works for you as supplementary material or for your own weekend learning curriculum. The books are sorted by grade from first to twelfth, but you are the teacher of your child. Use what you like.

You can also find other sources that are fee-based to help your child learn the Qur'an and Arabic. Your local library is also a good place to check for cultural learning materials, and if they do not have any you can request or recommend the library get certain books or online databases you might be interested in. For the Arabic language, there is an online program called Transparent Language that might be helpful, and once you sign up, you can also download its app to your phone or iPad. The program is free using your library card. These are supplemental materials, and as always you need to find a teacher of your choice to make sure your child is learning the basics of Islam: the five pillars, Seerah, books of hadith like the 40th hadith, Riyad As-saliheen, and also the Tafseer translation of the Qur'an.

My final recommendations for the weekend school are to connect with the teachers, know who is teaching your child, and also volunteer at the classes. Believe me, your presence makes a big difference. You will see the struggles the teachers are facing as well as the struggles that your children are having and what you can do about them. Form a parent group and discuss issues that concern you and your children. Remember, back home we relied on our teachers, but in the diaspora you have to be a proactive parent in your child's life whether it is for school during the week or on the weekend. If something happens tomorrow (may Allah forbid), you as a parent are going to answer to the authorities, and you will face pain on your own.

Take Charge of Your Child's Education

Today, we can see from our classrooms that teachers are frustrated and behavioral issues are overtaking their teaching time! Many schools are using grants to reduce behavior problems in the classroom, which gives teachers a break and time to teach students. However, the students with behavior issues may be missing instruction that is happening in the main classroom. Some teachers have even begun using a character education curriculum in the classroom.

As a parent, you are responsible for your children. That can mean education, nutrition, safety, or environment. You are also the mentor, the motivator, and the teacher. Remember, the phrase "parenting style" comes from observations of parents who were with their young children. I would like you to think of quality in everything you want for your children. Now think of how you can be involved in your child's school or dugsi, motivate them, feed them with quality food, and help them learn life skills.

Life skills are critical to education. Your child needs a good character to interact with people. Many teachers and coaches expect parents to instill good character in their children and send them to school acting like an angel. Well, we know that without a good character, it is hard to follow directions, learn something beneficial, and deal with people. You can help your child get the most out of their education by getting involved in their schools and activities. In Islam, you are the person solely responsible for your child. Yes, ideally society is responsible at some point, but we, parents, are the ones who work with the society, schools, dugsi, community centers, and so on.

There are many strategies that parents can use to build their children's character. These include role modeling, storytelling, and doing community/volunteer work. Of course, the first priority is to be a role model for your child. For example, if you tell your child that lying is not good and one day he hears you talking on the phone and doing what you told him not to do, you will be ineffective. You can also intentionally introduce one habit at a time. Helping others is a habit that the whole family can demonstrate. Schedule a visit with a teacher after school, for example, and help clean her room.

Storytelling is an amazing tool that you can use to teach your own values and traditions as well as other people's culture. Read the biography of Prophet Muhammad (peace be upon him) and choose a story that has a habit you want to teach. Read together and discuss it. For example, "Trustworthy," or Al-Amen, was a nickname for the Prophet. Ask your child how one can be trustworthy. Today, we use this term for job references, and it is something that employers value. You cannot pretend to be trustworthy, and developing trust takes time. Pick story books that talk about empathy, cooperation, kindness, and shared values like the "Golden Rule." The Golden Rule is my favorite because it eliminates some concepts that our children pick up randomly. For example, our children are confused when we teach them the hadith that talks about "being nice to your neighbors." The majority of them assume that we have to be nice to Somali or Muslim neighbors only. They do not see adults interact with neighbors who are not Somali or Muslim very often.

Working or volunteering in the community is also a great way to teach good character. The volunteer work is not paid, and your child will learn that sometimes we do not need to ask for money for the work we do for our community. This is becoming a skill that schools are using nowadays too. You will see some high schools and colleges require completion of certain volunteer hours in your community. In fact, this can sometimes lead to great opportunities like scholarships.

Having a good character is not only going to help our children in the academic world, it is good for everyone, including you as a parent. The teachers in the classroom will help your child learn well, you will be happy when he is less defiant, and people will like and want to help him. Good character is a transferable skill that will be with your child for the rest of his life.

We need to understand that an imam can be a dugsi teacher, but not all dugsi teachers are imams. Similarly, a masjid can be a dugsi, but not all dugsis are masjids. I am sure one of the main reasons we, Somali parents, are shipping away our "terrible teens" is because of the lack of character education. It is important for parents to understand this because when incidents happen in weekend dugsi, they quickly think that the imam, or the leader of that mosque if the dugsi was in a mosque, has to do with what happened. This can be a fight between two kids or an abuse that happened in the dugsi. So, an imam can sometimes be a dugsi teacher, and a dugsi can be run in any building. So, know who the teacher and administrator are when you are enrolling your child in a weekend dugsi. In this case, if something happens, you know who to call or talk to without pointing fingers at the masjid, because the masjid is for the entire community, not an individual!

When it comes to character, we are not alone. American schools are in need of good character education programs. We, parents, are powerful if we use our strengths together. We need to work with the rest of our American fellows to make our schools a place where children learn about good character as they grow up.

Sexual Abuse

Sexual abuse is becoming the silent killer of our youth and children. Discussion of sex and sex education is taboo and suppressed in the community. Most abuse that is happening is caused by lack of awareness of the rights of women and children, and predators in the community are taking advantage of this silence and using their power to rape and assault women and children.

I hear stories of sexual abuse from concerned parents, especially mothers, and as a mother and a member of the Somali community, it bothers me a lot. I am from a community that stigmatizes mental illness and discussion of abuse of any kind toward women and children. One day I asked one of my friends out of curiosity and courage, "How do we know if young children are getting abused?" I wanted her opinion since she had small children and we were talking about teenage boys and girls being sexually abused. Her answers shocked me and at the same time gave me hope that Somali parents are very concerned about their children's safety and care about their education and upbringing. But one thing that we are missing is a way to get help or equip our children with the right tools.

"So," the mother said to me, "You know, Ruqia, if someone sexually abuses girls it is bad, but if it happens to boys it is very bad."

I asked, "Why very bad?"

She said, "Because he is a boy and will lack his manhood when he grows up. To prevent that, every time my son comes home, I go with him to the bathroom and wash him [in Islam we have to wash after using the restroom]. If he says "ouch" then I know something happened to him. I look at the area for redness and I start asking him more questions and take him out of that learning place."

Another painful story I heard about, that happened several years ago, was when a woman suspected that her husband was abusing her daughter when she went to work. One day, her daughter came back from school, and the mother left the house pretending that she was off to work. The mother waited a few minutes, entered the house, heard her daughter screaming in another room, and saw with her own eyes that her husband was raping her daughter! The mother started screaming and the husband ran away!

The final story I want to share is, a mother discovered that her baby was unusually coughing and throwing up after she came back from work. She asked her babysitter, who was a friend, what food she gave the baby and what happened. The babysitter answered only milk. The mother called 911, and pediatricians performed tests. The lab results showed that the substance the baby was throwing up was semen! The babysitter confessed that she briefly left the baby with her boyfriend when she left to get something from the grocery store!

Well, these and similar stories brought my attention to the abuse that is happening, and yes, parents are aware of it. Of course, these predators didn't all get away with their crimes, but my worry is the psychological damage they caused to the families and children.

It is also difficult to discuss the subject because we live in a community that, for instance, tells a mother who lost her teen in a boarding school that if she tells the authorities about the death of her son, she will be arrested!

We have a lot of room for improvement when it comes to protecting our children and educating ourselves about what to do when things go wrong.

These children and youth are our future leaders. If we do not protect them both individually and collectively, we will have chaos in society. Many abortions happen to our high school girls, and due to our culture that silences girls by shaming them, girls continue to hide sexual assault and abuse, and boys continue to harass girls!

We need short- and long-term solutions to our problems. No one is going to come and solve this for us. Also, Allah is not going to change our condition until we decide to change it.

I have a few recommendations and hope as a parent you will come up with your own strategies as well.

- Teach your children, boys and girls, that their body is their body and no one else's.

- Make sure that your daughters do not hang out with non-Mahrams (those men that can marry).
- As a parent, learn signs of child abuse and document what your child says as well as what you saw, when you saw it, and who was involved.

Many of our children do not know what is a good touch or a bad touch. We can teach these skills in schools and community centers. Depending on the age of the children, we can use developmentally appropriate language and show demonstrations of what bad touching looks like. We also need to reassure children because those predators use threatening language when they abuse. They may say, "If you tell anyone what I did, I will kill you or kill your family."

When children get this confidence from you, they will have the courage to communicate who is abusing them no matter who that person is. This is true with older teens too. When something goes wrong in a teen's life and they do not have someone to turn to, they will act out and that will spill into their academics and other aspects of their life. Sometimes as parents, we assume that the teen is disobedient when they talk back, but sometimes they act wild and confused because of abuse that is happening or frustration they have with someone else. Make sure that you reconnect with your teen as soon as you feel the relationship is in jeopardy.

We, Somali people, value tribes and kinship, and these are not bad if they are used for good. We use the word "cousin" a lot, to the point that our children are confused as to how many cousins we have. The majority of us also live together, so when a relative comes to your state or city, you feel obliged to host them until they find an apartment or go back after visiting.

Now, the tricky question is "To host or not to host," and I will say use your judgement! Most abuse comes from close relatives, and nowadays with all the use of drugs like Shiisha and other substances, I am hearing about Mahrams who are intoxicated abusing children and youth! You may be raising your eyebrows and thinking that is HARAM. Well I want you to also think who said drugs are HALAL, because using haram leads to haram, and I do not think an intoxicated person will know what religion he has and whether the person standing in front of him is his child or wife!

As a parent, you are responsible for what happens to your child, and it is your responsibility to always pay attention to the signs of child abuse. There are several signs of child abuse depending on what kind of abuse is happening.

According to the Mayo Clinic, symptoms of sexual abuse include trouble walking or sitting, blood in the underwear, and sex conversations that are not appropriate for the age of the child (2018). Some of the children may resist, and the predator may use physical abuse at this time. The child will exhibit defiant behavior problems and try to run away from home or school, especially when boys are abused if the abuse is happening at school. Some men will even go to learning centers to hunt children. So, if your child shows a sudden change in behavior, stop and think!

Failure to protect your child will not only give the abuser more chances to abuse other children, it will also create mistrust between you and your child. If others figure out what happened and report it, or your child reports it, you will be in trouble legally. Also, since Allah entrusted you with these children, you will be asked about this on the Day of Judgement!

Treatment of Boys versus Girls

Our treatment of boys and girls culturally is contributing to many of the problems children are facing today in our communities. We used to have different roles in a different time and environment, and implementing the same old method is not working.

As we know, we used to perform female genital mutilation to girls for several reasons. FGM was a protective factor for girls against rape! It made it difficult for men to easily have sex and go. Girls, according to the old saying, are like meat, and men are the hyenas. My point is, as we saw in 2017, there were a lot of women speaking up against sexual harassment. We see in the news hashtags like #metoo and #timesup; I am still waiting for when Somalis will say #timesup for domestic violence and stop biding our time and thinking that being patient with an abusive relationship will lead us to heaven. We have a long way to go with talking about sexual harassment!

As parents we know that there has been a big backlash about FGM, and in Minnesota there is a bill on the floor that is asking legislators to make it illegal and to hold anyone who does this to children accountable.

Another thing we are doing is having our girls do the housework and letting boys focus on their studies and what they are going to major in. What does not make sense is that we are doing this unconsciously without realizing that the role boys used to play was to do all the outside work.

Boys were also responsible for protecting women and girls, NOT exploiting and abusing them as we are witnessing in the diaspora!

CHAPTER SIX

Resources: Human and Materials

We are finishing our book with a chapter that will hopefully give you, as a parent, tools that you can use along the way. We will highlight how to cultivate a network of people, friends as well as professionals, that you can use as a support system.

In 2002, I had my second child in the United States. The first night in the hospital, I woke up early and realized I was alone in the room, so I pushed the bottom for help. When the nurse entered the room, I looked her in the eyes and said, "Where is my baby?" She told me that he was in the nursery and they wanted me to rest and sleep well. I said, "No thank you, I want him in my room." She brought him to the room, and I nursed him and kissed my baby.

Around lunchtime, the doctor came into the room and started chatting with me for a while. She then said, "Let me show you where the nurses care for babies while the mothers sleep."

She showed me the area, and I asked, "But how am I going to know which one is my baby?" Seriously, all of them seemed to have the same faces to me.

"They have their parents' name on their wrists," she said, smiling. We went back to the room, and she said, "You are a good mother and love your baby so much, but remember, if you really want to give your child good care, first start caring for yourself. Then you will have more energy to care for him!"

I never forgot those words and try to apply them to every aspect of parenting.

There are people at certain points in our lives whose value and importance we do not always recognize. They act as mentors to us whether we realize it or not. I have a mentor at my workplace as well as outside of work. It is not necessary that these mentors or coaches are official; what matters is that you reach out to them when you need help and that they are there for you.

The Importance of Having a Support System

Building a support system and a network is an important task for us as Somali parents living in the diaspora! We might already have some sort of support system in the United States, but may not be aware of it at all!

For example, the personal story I shared at the beginning of this section says a lot about our living conditions as parents and the lack of trust we have in the system and society we live in! I was not aware of that small service during my hospital stay, and it meant a lot to me. We all carry our biases and will even decline a service because we don't trust who is offering that service. We might also think that declining services is linked to a lack of educational background, but in reality, it has to do with trust and understanding of the system.

Personally, I never had a language issue when I came to this country. My parents made sure that I learned English at a young age. I started working for the United Nations in Somalia as a teenager, and that happened because of my language skills.

I also did not have a phobia of foreign people, including non-Muslims. My grandfather (may Allah have mercy on him) was a chef for an Italian company that used to export bananas from Somalia, and he used to take us to his job outside of the city. So we ate with many different people—and in 1994, my first job at the American Embassy in Somalia exposed me to foreign workers, and I viewed diversity as a good thing.

However, in this particular case, sometimes it is difficult to accept services, different situations, and systems of education that we never had back home. Healthcare was totally foreign to me, and I needed time to digest and accept it.

It is also important to understand that no matter what you study, there is always an unconscious way of life that we have inside, and it can come out of us unconsciously when things happen. That is why we have unconscious bias trainings after employees exhibit hidden and unconscious behaviors toward their customers.

I used to see my mother and others have their babies close to them. Babies slept in the same bed as the mothers (safety and sudden infant death syndrome is not what we are talking about). Even when I had my first daughter in Pakistan, I do not remember going to another room besides my own. Whether that is good or bad, it was the way I had learned from my observations, and I had to implement that knowledge as I become a mother.

It is equally important that we mention what else I used to observe that I do not observe here in the diaspora! Whenever my mother, or one of our relatives, had a baby, neighbors and relatives visited the house and divided up the chores. Some washed the mother's clothes, some cooked for the rest of the family, and some held the baby on their lap so the mother could rest or take brief naps between the frequent visitations that occurred in the first few days after the delivery! The mother also made arrangements for these expected visitations and called her network of friends to come a few days before the due date, to clean the house and make some sweet treats and OOTKAC, a small cube of meat fried in oil, to serve guests. So, social support was in full function, and it was not necessarily a written structure but an assumed and followed tradition we received from our ancestors!

Here, in the United States, this tradition is disappearing due to circumstances surrounding the immigrant families. In my story it became more clear to me as years passed and I reflected upon our situation. There are some social support systems that the diaspora offers, but we do not know about them, or they seem strange, and we do not take help immediately. We need time and the right environment to digest everything in order to have trust in the system and the societal structure.

As a Somali parent in the diaspora, you may relate to my story or have another amazing and relevant story that could ring true to our situation. The world is changing in dramatic ways, such as the way we communicate, the way we do business, and the way our children are growing up. In order to combat this and become successful, we need to build relationships with others. We do not need to reinvent the wheel, but make connections and rediscover what is already available to us and enhance or modify it to meet our particular situations. Sometimes there are great opportunities and services available to us, but we simply do not know where they are and who to ask. Creating a network of people can be a good starting point to building perennial and professional relationships that enhance our parenting process.

Building a Social Support System That Will Help Us Survive and Thrive

The social support system we used to have a long time ago has diminished, and we need to rediscover it while at the same time reinventing new methods that will help us survive and thrive here in the diaspora. Somali parents need a conducive environment that allows them to learn new things without pressure, practice their positive cultural aspects, and interact with others.

We relied on our neighbors and extended family members before, and they did a great job embracing the task of parenting as a community responsibility. However, now and in the diaspora, things have totally changed. The social system is different, and that may be the main reason we as immigrants and refugees came here. Somali parents understand fully what I am talking about, but due to feelings of shame and internalization of the oppression, we hide things, and everything we hide hunts us sooner or later! That, in turn, impacts our parenting experience.

Parents need to develop trust in and understanding of the systems of the social structure they live in. They also need to effectively judge the trustworthiness of extended family members, friends, and neighbors before they trust them. Some parents who thought the support system we used back home is still working here in the diaspora have learned their lesson after they experienced problems.

In 2009, a Somali man living in Kansas sexually assaulted and impregnated his stepdaughter, and his wife was found dead. The story is frightening and complex. According to the gossip we heard, the young girl complained to her mother that her uncle was sexually assaulting her! The mother tried everything she could think of to solve the situation. She contacted the local religious leaders, talked to the uncle, and filed a complaint. Long story short, the girl become pregnant, and the situation escalated until the mother was found dead.

This story and similar stories remind us that the old system and trust of close relatives need to be reconsidered in the diaspora! This may be scary and can create suspicions among people who behave well, but the main point is to understand as parents that if something goes wrong in this country, even you as a parent can go to jail if you are proven to be an abuser! Some parents are too dangerous to be with children and in this case, a relative may be a safe haven or vice versa!

Building Support and Network Relations

The Qur'an says, "Indeed, Allah will not change the condition of a people until they change what is in themselves" (13:11). Somali parents are in a state of confusion because of a new environment and system that we do not know or do not trust. Of course, we did not choose to be in this situation from the beginning. Circumstances such as trauma and migration are the cause. However, once we are settled in the new land we now call home, it becomes almost obligatory to learn the new system of living and surviving. It is clear from the verse in the Qur'an—Allah will not change our condition until we make an effort to change it. We need to be proactive in learning new things, enhancing our knowledge, and modifying our old way of living to accommodate our new generation, our beloved children, whose lives we are working very hard day and night to improve!

In this part, I will help you develop a system to create a personal, parental, and professional network and support system. First, understand that in any situation, personal or societal, there are three levels of preventive measures. These can help when you are trying to handle or improve the condition of any situation. The levels are:

1. Primary prevention
2. Secondary prevention
3. Tertiary prevention

An example of primary prevention is maintaining the

overall wellness of a situation. Your child is in school and he is maintaining his grades, reading well at his grade level, and doing his homework without needing much help. Secondary prevention is when the child is performing below his grade level or is at risk of failing. The third level, tertiary, is when the child fails or flunks a grade and has to repeat it. In other words, the first level is ideal and what we strive for, and the third level is when problems happen and we are in crisis mode!

As you create your own support system, remember the three levels of prevention and apply them to your own unique situation. For example, if your situation is at the secondary, or risk, level, pull out a list for that situation and reach out. Similarly, if you need somewhat urgent help for your parenting process, or have a child who is really acting weird or getting more Cs, reach out to your crisis team.

Parental and Professional Network

Building a parental and professional network helps you have a support system and use it when needed. We all have relationships with friends, neighbors, relatives, and some professional individuals. We need to put them into a categorized list and enhance our relationship with them while we of course keep growing our list. To start out, first look at your personal contact list. We all need social time, and that is when we reach out to those individuals who care most about what matters to us. Make two lists: parental and professional. Put all the names of parents in the PARENT list and the people who are care providers, doctors, social workers, librarians, and youth workers in the PROFESIONAL list. Make sure to update this list every six months. Do the same thing with people that you are friends with on social media and who are local. Ask the parents that are responsive if they can chat with you about finding parent workshop classes and discuss the learning and growth of your children. The meetings can happen at libraries, community centers, or even at the mosques.

Start planning to talk to the people on your professional list one at a time and ask questions about children's programs and parent classes. For example, you can talk to your children's doctor or your own when you are visiting the clinic and a librarian when you are visiting the library. Remember, the goal is to be proactive and build network relations. By the time you really need help about a children's or family issue, reaching out to those individuals will feel comfortable because you made connections with them already! The librarian may tell you about upcoming children's programs and the social worker may tell you about educational opportunities or programs in the community that serve families and children. You can even invite one of those professional individuals to your parent gatherings!

You will reach a stage when you are so excited you cannot wait until the next meeting. Then it is time to add cultural-style events and schedule a monthly potluck with parents. You can even invite other parents to be allies and support your efforts to bring parents together to discuss the future of your children. Make sure to ask people if there are any workshops for parents that are happening in your city. Attend those workshops even if the language is not easy, and make connections with other parents that are not from East Africa. We live in a world that is diverse, and when it comes to caring for and educating our children, we have one goal no matter what our background is. That goal is to give our children the best possible educational opportunity we can!

Alle Barri Time!

Alle is "Allah" and Barri is "pray" or "ask." It is an old tradition that families used to do in which they hosted a feast and prayed to and praised Allah! Some rare families do it in the diaspora, and the goal and intention seem to be the same. I love to pray, as many others do, whenever something is uncomfortable. The majority of people remember to pray when things are in crisis mode. We see this in the media; for example, whenever a shooting happens, people offer their prayers to the victims. Sending thoughts and prayers is a common phrase we hear nowadays due to the unstoppable tragedies we are witnessing. Traditionally, we did not wait for something bad to happen in order to say prayers or Alle Barri.

During my childhood, I used to see it happening in our home too. The family invites or hosts about a hundred or so guests such as other families, relatives, neighbors, religious leaders, and yes, the beggars. A large amount of food gets cooked in the house by some talented ladies and the meat is from at least two goats if not a whole cow! After eating the food, people pray for family members, including children. Religious leaders read some portions of the Qur'an and pray too. My favorite part of this is when the close neighbors take food home and several beggars gather outside the house and wait for food. How did they get the invitation? Well, whenever such Alle Barri is happening, you will notice two things: a large number of people going back and forth to that particular house and the blood stains and the skins of the slaughtered animal are visible.

We do not have to do that big feast here in the diaspora, but we need to do prayers at all times. As we start our tasks in the parenting process, it may seem difficult. Some parents may say my children or my child are already in jail or have failed in school and I do not have a chance. No, the doors of Allah are always open. So, as you build your support system and make changes, make the Alle Barri part of your task. Modify it; you can turn your monthly potluck to Alle Barri and distribute the food to the homeless and the needy people. Make people happy by buying some surprise gifts for a child who did not get a chance to have caring parents as you care for your children. Even if the child does not say prayers that you can hear, the happy heart will pray for you!

Acknowledgments

All thanks is due to Allah, who endowed me with the knowledge, experiences, and insights that I am sharing with you.

I am very thankful for my father, Aden Ali, and mother, Khadija Osman, who both gave me the best nurturing a child can have! I learned a lot from them about raising confident and compassionate children. Above all, I wouldn't be the mama bear and the educated mother I am without my mother. My mother instilled in me good character and allowed me to receive the best early education a child can have.

I also wouldn't be the the brave butterfly I am without receiving encouragement and freedom from my father, who treated me no different than boys, especially when girls are treated differently in the Somali culture!

Nobody has been more important to me in the pursuit of this project than my family: my husband, Mohamed Mohamoud, and my three children. Thank you for being supportive and patient!

I owe a debt of gratitude to my publisher, the Wise Ink team: Laura Zats, who coached me in every stage of the book. My editor, Erik, who made suggestions that were so essential and at times tough to accept, but worth taking. Patrick and Graham for their amazing help in terms of book design and its contributions. Roseanne, who carefully crafted my wording through edits. You do not want to go to the market without Roseanne!

As always, it's nice to have cheerleaders around me, like Bernie Farrell, Youth Services Coordinator of Hennepin County Library, and Sarah Super, the founder of Break the Silence, who also introduced me to this amazing publisher, Wise Ink. I cannot forget to mention the positive attitude and encouragement I received from Amelia Hansa, the coordinator of the Best Buy Teen Center in Minneapolis Central Library. Your ideas were useful!

I would love to give exceptional thanks to all parents, especially mothers, who shared their stories with me. Stories from parents inspired me not only to write this book about parenting issues, but also discuss what caused Somali parents of the diaspora to reach this stage and to point out to all parties that they can have a stake in the journey of better parenting! It has been incredibly helpful to me, and I was able to reflect while simultaneously writing this milestone book that I hope will be a game changer for teachers, counselors, and coaches, and for Somali parents!

I hope this book is going to change the way Somali parents experience parenting and the way service providers serve the Somali Community.

References

The American Academy of Pediatrics. 2012. "Breastfeeding and the Use of Human Milk." Pediatrics 129, no. 3 (Mar. 2012): https://doi.org/10.1542/peds.2011-3552.

Berge, Jerica M., Melanie Wall, Katherine W. Bauer, and Dianne Neumark-Sztainer. "Parenting Characteristics in the Home Environment and Adolescent Overweight: A Latent Class Analysis." *Obesity* 18.4 (2010): 818-825.

Carskadon, Mary. "Inside the Teenage Brain." n.d. Frontline. PBS. https://www.pbs.org/wgbh/pages/frontline/shows/teenbrain/interviews/carskadon.html.

Center on the Developing Child. n.d. "5 Steps for Brain-Building Serve and Return." Harvard University. https://developingchild.harvard.edu/resources/5-steps-for-brain-building-serve-and-return

"Child Abuse." 2018. Mayo Clinic. https://www.mayoclinic.org/diseases-conditions/child-abuse/symptoms-causes/syc-20370864.

Connor, Phillip, and Jens Manuel Krogstad. 2016. "5 Facts About the Global Somali Diaspora." Pew Research Center. http://www.pewresearch.org/fact-tank/2016/06/01/5-facts-about-the-global-somali-diaspora/.

Dolch, Edward W. 1948. *Problems in Reading.* Champaign, IL: Garrard Press.

Dweck, Carol S. 2016. *Mindset: The New Psychology of Success.* New York: Random House.

National Academies of Sciences, Engineering, and Medicine. 2016. *Parenting Matters: Supporting Parents of Children Ages 0–8.* Edited by Vivian L. Gadsden, Morgan Ford, and Heather Breiner. Washington D.C.: The National Academies Press. https://doi.org/10.17226/21868.

Hadith. n.d. Sunnah.com. http://www.sunnah.com.

Heitner, Devorah. 2016. *Screenwise: Helping Kids Thrive (and Survive) in Their Digital World.* Brookline, MA: Bibliomotion, Inc.

"Huuwaya Huuwa Somali Baby Song Somali Lullaby." YouTube. November 2, 2016. www.youtube.com/watch?v=YT_YhesfxOk&feature=youtu.be.

Kendra Cherry. "The 4 Stages of Cognitive Development: Background and Key Concepts of Piaget's Theory." Verywell mind. About, Inc. (Dotdash). Updated October 15, 2018. www.verywell.com/piagets-stages-of-cognitive-development-2795457.

Klein, Helen Altman, and Jeanne Ballantine. 2001. "For Parents Particularly: Raising Competent Kids: The Authoritative Parenting Style." Childhood Education 78 (1): 46–47. https://doi.org/10.1080/00094056.2001.1052168 9.

Mitchell, Corey. "Immigrant Influxes Put U.S. Schools to the Test." Education Week 35, no. 24: 10-11. Updated March 30, 2016. https://www.edweek.org/ew/articles/2016/03/16/immigrant-influxes-put-us-schools-to-test.html.

Mubārakfūrī, Safi-'r-Rahmān al-, and Abdul Malik Mujahid. *The Sealed Nectar: (Ar-Raheequl-Makhtum) ; Biography of the Noble Prophet*. Maktaba Dar-us-Salam, 1995.

Muennig, Peter, Dylan Robertson, Gretchen Johnson, Frances Campbell, Elizabeth P. Pungello, and Matthew Neidell. 2011. "The Effect of an Early Education Program on Adult Health: The Carolina Abecedarian Project Randomized Controlled Trial." American Journal Of Public Health 101 no. 3 (March 2011): 512-516. https://doi.org/10.2105/AJPH.2010.200063.

National Association for the Education of Young Children. 2009. "Developmentally Appropriate Practice in Early Childhood Programs Serving Children from Birth through Age 8: Position Statement." National Association for the Education of Young Children. https://www.naeyc.org/sites/default/files/globally-shared/downloads/PDFs/resources/position-state-ments/PSDAP.pdf.

Norrman, Gunnar, and Emanuel Bylund. 2016. "The Irreversibility of Sensitive Period Effects in Language Development: Evidence from Second Language Acquisition in International Adoptees." Developmental Science 19 no.3 (May 2016): 513-520. https://doi.org/10.1111/desc.12332

Quran. 2016. The Noble Quran. http://www.quran.com.

Ragelienė, Tija. "Links of Adolescents Identity Development and Relationship with Peers: A Systematic Literature Review." *Journal of the Canadian Academy of Child and Adolescent Psychiatry* 25.2 (2016).

Santori, Mathew, and Maureen Wagner. 2013. "Early Childhood Development Services in Cedar-Riverside: Landscape Analysis and Strategic Action Plan." (Master of Public Policy Professional Paper, The University of Minnesota). https://conservancy.umn.edu/bitstream/handle/11299/149292/santori_?sequence=1.

Shah, Saqib. 2016. "The History of Social Networking." Digital Trends. www.digitaltrends.com/features/the-history-of-social-networking/.

"What Are the Benefits of Breastfeeding?" Eunice Kennedy Shriver National Institute of Child Health and Human Development. U.S. Department of Health and Human Services. Last reviewed July 27, 2018. www.nichd.nih.gov/health/topics/breastfeeding/condition-info/Pages/benefits.aspx.